Dalits of Nepal

Issues and Challenges

Dalits of Nepal
Issues and Challenges

Compiled and Edited by
Prabodh M. Devkota

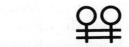

Feminist Dalit Organization (FEDO)
Kupondole, Lalitpur

Dalits of Nepal
Issues and Challenges
Published by
Feminist Dalit Organization (FEDO)
Kupondole, Lalitpur, Nepal
P.O. Box 4366 Kathmandu, Nepal
Tel: 520982, 543986
e-mail: dms@fedo.wlink.com.np

© FEDO, 2005

Re-Print 1000 Copy

ISBN 99933-384-0-0

All prepress technical assistance except editing for this publication is voluntarily contributed by Mr. Madhab Lal Maharjan, Mandala Book Point, Kantipath, Kathmandu, Nepal, e-mail: books@mos.com.np;mandala @ccsl.com.np

Printed & Layout by
Anup Offset Press
Pulchowk, Lalitpur
Tel.: 5523117

Publisher's Note

Feminist Dalit Organization (FEDO) was founded in 1994. It is the first and the only organization of its type in the whole nation, which represents the Dalit Women, their voices, their concerns, and addresses their needs.

Even after the restoration of the Democracy, Dalit and Dalit women's situation has remained unchanged. Their political, economic and social conditions are still dominated by the illness of caste discrimination. In this context, the situation of the mass Nepali women is miserable and the situation of Dalit women is even more deplorable. They suffer from both caste and gender discriminations.

Our voice are neglected in the mainstream politics and in the main stream written history. There are no more books that reflect the historical value of the Dalit community and their contribution to the state. In this context, we believe, the book entitled *"Dalits of Nepal: Issues and Challenges"* has tried to explore some realities that will be helpful for the better understanding of the issues of the Dalits in Nepal. This attempt is the first step towards a long journey.

We are grateful to Mr. Prabodh M. Devkota, the editor of the book who has produced the book after a long and constant struggle. His rold was vital for the production of this book, we must appreciate his effort. We would like to express our appreciation and sincere thanks to the scholars whocontributed for the production of the book by providing their highly valuable articles. At the same time we would like to give our sincere thanks to the Royal Danish Embassy and Lutheran World Federation for their financial support to publish the book. Similarly we would like to thank Danida/ DASU for financial support to re-print the book.

Feminist Dalit Organization (FEDO)
Publisher

Editor's Note

After a long and constant effort we have been able to bring the book entitled *"Dalits of Nepal: Issues and Challenges"* before the readers. This is the collection of writings by different writers from Nepal and abroad on the issues and subject of the Dalits of Nepal. I do not want to claim that this book will be a unique work of its kind but I do certainly believe that it will introduce some academic issues that are concerned with the Dalits in the Nepalese context.

I am thankful to FEDO, the publisher of the book, for giving me the responsibility of an editor. I am thankful to Dr. Abhi Subedi who from the beginning to the end of this work has advised and inspired me to organise and bring the materials in this form. He has also read several texts over and given advice. Prof. Subedi's co-operation, therefore, has been very instrumental in this work.

I translated some Nepali articles. The articles that were made available to me have been included but I have also selected several other essays with an intention to look at the issues from different perspectives. I have realised that there are a number of other issues that had to be left out due to the constraints of both time and economy. We will try to present them in the next endeavour of this nature.

I am very thankful to all those writers who have helped us with articles and suggestions, at the same time I am also thankful to Prof. Shreedhar Lohani, Dr. Krishna B. Bhattachan and Dr. Arun Gupto for their precious suggestions.

I am also grateful to Mr. Madhab Lal Maharjan of Mandala Book Point for his technical suggestions.

Lalitpur, 1st February, 2002

Editor

Contents

Introduction

The issues concerning the minorities have appeared significantly on the agenda of the global discourses. Everywhere, everybody from politician to a layman, from social analyst to the journalist is talking about 'issues' today. At the same time, the issues of ethnicity, gender, caste, national culture and nationalism have prominently shaken the world of politics, economy, media and academic studies.

In the Nepalese context, the issue of Dalit[1] has become one of the powerful agenda related to culture, politics, media and economy. In every country there are segments of society who suffer from the process of marginalisation, suppression and oppression because each society is founded on the basic structure of power and politics. The power-holders on the basis of cultural, economic and political powers dominate the people who are suppressed. Power has its own dynamics; it is not static. At the same time both the suppresser and the suppressed are the equal parts in the structure of power relation. So there is a constant struggle between these groups. That is why there is a possibility of change in the process of history. And the same pattern can be seen in the context of

---

1 The literal meaning of Dalit is the person who is suppressed. In the context of South Asia, Dalit is a common term used to address the culturally, economically & socially marginalized people or community whereas in the context of Nepal, generally the word Dalit means a community or a person who suffers from the illness of caste discrimination.

the Dalits too. For some years Dalits are actively trying to seek their identities, their rights and find their social dignity.

I have always tried to look at the issues of Dalit from the point of view of a media person as well as an academician. Working with the media has given me first hand accessibility to look at the problems of the margins, and academics provides me epistemological insights. My research and knowledge about such issues come from my belief in media-academic complementarity. Working as a media person and conceptualizing as a teacher through debates and discussions in the classrooms, I strongly believe that the margins can articulate the experiences they go through. Subalterns can speak because these sections of society live and communicate with sufferings and pain. The best part of language is always derived from the intensity of experiences whether they are pain or pleasure. They can speak because one can see that they can speak their emotions and feelings in simple and ordinary languages. What such writings and books do is to imitate the language of the margins. If the imitation is honest, the original voices can always be heard.

This book tries to focus on the multiple aspects associated with the Dalits. Despite the constitutional equity Dalits as the mass Nepali citizens, remain at a level where their experiences are bitter. The entire Dalits suffer from the malady of caste discrimination. The reality of Dalit women is even more problematic, more delicate and more serious. The plight of the Dalit women is that they suffer from the double suppression of gender and caste discriminations. They suffer both within the community and outside of the community.

The book tries to focus on Dalit women and their conditions with major emphasis and the Dalit community and social responses in general. It tries to highlight their positions in the domains of education, law, male hegemony and economic independence. At the same time, scholars have tried to highlight on the socio-political, economic, and cultural realties of the entire Dalit communities with their research based findings and analysis.

Art and culture has become one of the richest modes of heritage in human history. Nepal has a unique cultural texture where dozens of cultural practices do co-exist, and are practised in everyday life. Music has its own place of importance in such cultural formation. Dalit communities seem to be the original promoters of the culture and the structuralism of music and performing arts in Nepal. Writers in the book have tried to explore the relationship of the Dalit community and music from the early Vedic times to the present especially in the domain of performance art in the region, and have made some important findings as regards the relationship of the Dalits of Nepal with the performance arts.

Representation has become one of the biggest issues throughout the world. Who represents whom is a major question. For example, we can ask questions like-- can the white community represent the black community? Can the non-Dalit community represent the Dalit community? Or, within the Dalit community can the upper class Dalit represent the lower class Dalit? Questions like these are still unsolved and they remain serious issues concerning the human development. Scholars in the book have tried to analyse the issue of representation in the context of Dalit community in Nepal.

Most often it is said that the national history is always the history of the rulers. In reality every society, every community has its own history; even the unrecorded silent saga is a history of a different order. But when the question of written history comes, a certain politics that discriminates the marginalised voices comes up. Common people are marginalised from the main stream history. The book has tried to historicise the hidden history of the Dalit community who have contributed for the formation, perpetuation and the development of this nation. It has tried to record the historical movements of the Dalits. At the same time, it has tried to record many topics of the hidden Dalit historicity.

A section of the book presents some case studies of the people from the Dalit community who suffer from the ills of caste discrimination, and shows how people's creativity is handicapped by such discriminatory practices. At the same time some writers have presented the picture of the Dalit community through their difficult but successful stories.

Authors in the book have tried to discuss different issues of Dalit community from the socio-political, cultural and economic perspectives. This book is a modest attempt to put different forms of discourses concerning the predicaments and the issues of the Dalits in Nepal. The articles are written by various scholars, who are responsible for their own views, but on the whole a consensus among all the writers has emerged on these issues: Dalits are the marginalised people whose position has not been highlighted in the main structure of national discourses; Dalits are the very productive people whose contribution to the development of a national culture and indigenous cultures has always remain ignored; Dalits are the people whose bright, vibrant and creative response to life becomes manifest in their performance arts and Dalits form the important cultural and social texture of this society that is forcefully and deliberately ignored by the caste-ridden society. All writers also seem to agree that it is time the society woke up to the new reality, that of involving the Dalits in the main stream of the national culture and the development process.

Finally, we do not claim that this book is one monograph of research findings. Instead, it is the collection of different independent views written both by the Dalit and other scholars that have indicated at different possibilities of the study of the main issues and challenges of the Dalits of Nepal. So this book is a modest first attempt made towards fostering that kind of understanding.

Prabodh Mani Devkota

Part One
Power, History and Society

Dalits of Nepal:
Their Movement Now and Then

Hira Vishwakarma

Historical Background

As its diverse and extreme geographical and climatic conditions, Nepal, the only Hindu Kingdom in the world, has its caste hierarchy even more diverse and extreme. The main basis of the social system is based on the caste system. Within the same system its own fellow brothers and sisters are regarded as *Shudra* and untouchable, which usually does not prevail in any other religions in the world. This is the artifact of the traditional caste-ridden culture.

The so-called untouchables of Nepal are created by the Hindu religion. According to this religion, the creator of the world *Brahma*, created *Brahmin* from his mouth, *Kshetria* from his head, *Vaishya* from his thigh and *Shudra* from his feet. In this way, from the very beginning of the creation, the *Shudras* are shown to have originated from the disrespectful part of the body of the creator. During the time of extremely feudalistic society, the king (*Kshetrias*) used to rule the country with his might. The priest (*Brahmins*) propounded by the *Vedas*, the traders and farmers (*Vaishyas*) used to handle the economy of the country and *Shudras* had to serve all of these classes of people through menial works. The religion, therefore, treated *Shudras* as inferior human beings and the extreme case was that of untouchability. This system was more formalized and ritualized by some famous Hindu sages like *Bhrigu* who propounded rules and regulations and formed *Manushrimiti* which provided guidance to the kings and further enhanced the caste system.

Dalits Before the Unification of Nepal (6th – 17th Century)

In Nepal, though casteism prevailed since the *Lichhabi* regime, it was not taken as a basis of the rule because religion did not serve as the mainspring of the state rule.

History reveals that Buddhism was in bloom during that period though Hinduism was making its way slowly into the mainstream of society. Casteism started to have its roots deeper into the society during the Malla period as the Malla king of Kathmandu, Jayasthiti Malla formalized it under the law in the 14th century. To further enhance the caste system and formalize it as a part of the total system, Jayasthiti Malla even invited *Brahmins* from south India. The present kingdom of Nepal is said to have taken its shape from the Shah kings of Gorkha in the western part of Nepal. Casteism as a part of Hindu religion believed to have forged its way into the society since the rule of these Shah kings in Gorkha. Based on the caste system, King Ram Shah in the 17th century formalized the caste system and his judiciary. He seemed to be very much influenced by Jayasthiti Malla of Kathmandu valley.

On the basis of *Manushmriti*, casteism was made very strong and social moves of discriminatory nature were enacted. Since then, all the people belonging to lower castes or untouchables were forced to wear clothes made of sacks, wear snail shell in ears as ornament and eat in the earthen pots. More than that, they were not allowed to acquire property, construct comfortable houses, touch persons of higher castes, and were rather forced to live in filthy slums which is still prevalent in Kathmandu valley as the settlements of *Pode* and *Chyame* (sweeper and filth handler). They are found on the outskirts of city centers and the bank of Bishnumati river. The education was far beyond their reach, as they were not even allowed to listen to the *Vedas*. According to *Manushrimiti,* if they happen to listen the Vedas, their ears should be blocked by pouring melting hot lead. If they ever happen to read Vedas, their tongues should be taken out.

Though the people belonging to lower castes had to live a life inferior to animals, they acquired certain skills in making agricultural tools, weapons, ornaments, shoes, khukuri, singing songs, sewing cloths and so on.

Unification of Nepal and Role Played by Dalits (17th –18th Century)

When king Prithvi Narayan Shah of Gorkha started his unification movement of Nepal, the Dalits cooperated him with their souls and hearts. As stated earlier, they had acquired the skills of making weapons, sewing clothes and making shoes which became helpful for the missions of unification. People of higher castes considered such jobs both inferior and against the religion. Such skills could not be learnt within a short period at the time when there was no concept of formal schools as those of today. Therefore, the role of these people was very crucial during the unification process. If the blacksmiths had not made weapons, the tailors had not sewn clothes, the cobblers had not made shoes for the troops of Prithvi Narayan Shah fighting in the battle, he would not have been able to achieve the target of unification. The singing caste Gaine disseminated the information of war and spread patriotism through their songs by playing fiddle which is called *Sarangi* in Nepali. That is why, king Prithvi Narayan Shah had said, "Nepal is an orchard of four *Varnas* (components) and thirty-six castes, so has to be understood by all". In this way Dalits also played important role to strengthen the spirit of nationalism.

Bise Nagarchi the royal tailor of Prithvi Narayan Shah gave noble suggestions to raise one rupee from each 5000 households of Gorkha to purchase guns from Varanasi, at the time when royal treasury was empty and king himself was in confusion on the means of fund raising. Nagarchi himself gave one rupee first and initiated the movement.

Despite their contribution for the unification of Nepal, no successive efforts were put to uplift their conditions. On the contrary, the war prisoners and captives were degraded into untouchables resulting into increased number of untouchables. During and after the unification, the castes of some of the untouchables, who were able to please the rulers, were promoted into touchables. For instance, king Prithvi Narayan Shah himself changed the caste of an untouchable caste called Duwar to Putwar, Jung Bahadur Rana uplifted the hierarchy of Salmis and Bir Shumsher that of Nakarmis both from Newar community of Kathmandu valley.

Situation after
Muluki Ain (National Code) of 1853

The rule of nation was thus guided by Hinduism and was based on caste system under the feudalistic political system. In 1847, Jung Bahadur Kunwar (later promoted to Rana) took over the power through a bloody massacre of high-ranking officials of royal family and government. During his rule, Muluki Ain (National Code) was brought into effect in 1853. Some of the social evils like *Satipratha* - burning the wife alive on the pyre of her dead husband- and slavery were reformed by *Ain* though not banned completely. Unfortunately, the *Ain* further formalized the caste system and created atrocities for lower caste people, especially the untouchables. The following account will give a picture of such atrocities.

Since the beginning of the 14th century from the time of King Jayasthiti Malla of Kathmandu valley, the lower caste people, deprived of acquiring property, were forced to live in the fringes of upper caste settlements or in slums. Such filthy livings were the telling on their health; they became more careless on their cleanliness and dietary habits. Being Hindus, their entrance in the Hindu temples were denied and were not allowed to perform any rituals. The question of acquiring education during that period was a forgotten issue as the Brahmins had control over the entire education system. Not only that, the untouchables were not even allowed to involve them in social works like planting trees of religious importance, making platforms for taking rest in the shadow of tree, digging water ponds and so on. They were further deprived of attending festivals and fairs and even celebrating their marriages or arranging funerals like others.

For the similar kinds of crimes there were different punishments for different castes. For example, if a man from Brahmin caste had affairs with a lower caste woman, he would be outcasted and degraded to the caste of that woman. If a man of lower caste had an affair with an upper caste woman, he would be beheaded or sent into exile.

Walking on the same path, if a lower caste person happened to meet an upper caste person, he had to make way for the upper caste person and salute him saying *"Jadau"*. He was not supposed to carry a two-way conversation. When they accidentally touched the upper caste person the sprinkle of gold immersed water was required to purify the impurity caused by touching the lower caste. This system still prevails in many parts of the country and the severity of the problem can be seen in the Mid and Far Western parts of the country.

The same code of 1853 formalised the division of *Shudras* into two categories: one who could be enslaved or killed and the other who could not be enslaved or killed. All these untouchables were referred as Dalits.

In this way, the untouchables were living a severe life as they were facing social boycott and hatred from the upper caste people or being treated like criminals without committing crime as such.

Who are These Untouchables or Dalits?

The word Dalit literally means a person emerged from a swamp. As the Hindu religion has classified the castes into four groups as *Brahmin, Kshetria, Vaishya* and *Shudra*, the lowest group in that hierarchy, *Shudra*, has been termed as Dalit or untouchables. According to Hindu religion, one has to purify with gold treated water if s/he touches a *Shudra*.

Similarly, a dish has to be purified with a burning charcoal if it is used by an untouchable. A house of upper caste person has to be purified by chanting *mantras* of *Rudri* (a religious practice often performed to free the people of higher caste from evil spirits, which clearly indicates that untouchables are regarded as evils in the Hindu hierarchy of caste) if, by mistake, an untouchable enters the house.

The untouchables or Dalits of Nepal are slightly different from the Indian Dalits. As cross marriage took place during the time of early civilization, the color, complexion and blood do not help us to distinguish the touchables from the untouchables at a glance as one can differentiate between an African black and European white or Chinese origin of Mangol. Therefore, the question, "who are these untouchables?" remains unanswered. In the present context, none of the researches has been carried out by the concerned people or scholars to find out their origins and how they became untouchables. However, on the basis of their culture and social behavior, an effort has been made here to answer the aforementioned question.

We have a limited knowledge about the Dalits who have been living in the Terai belts of Nepal for centuries. Therefore, my attempt is more towards discussings about the Hill dwellers.

During the early civilisation of Nepal when Tibeto Burman people were ruling or staying in herds, casteism was not in practice. Casteism was introduced particularly after the entry of Hinduism as a foundation for the rule of the country.

Most of the Dalits follow Hinduism as their religion. Their rituals performed at the time of death, birth, marriage and other ceremonies are the same as that of the upper castes Hindus. Interesting enough, the surnames of these lower castes almost tally with the surnames of higher caste people. In many parts of Nepal, people with same surnames but belonging to upper caste and lower caste, live together. For instance, Brahmins with surname of Vashyal and untouchable Sarki with the same surname live in Takukot village of Gorkha district; Kshetrias with surname of Samarkhati and blacksmith with the same surname live in the same village of Gairagaon of Tansen town. Likewise, several such examples can be found in other parts of the country. All these evidences make it obvious that these untouchables were derailed from the hierarchy of the caste system due to various reasons which are subject to anthropological and sociological research and analysis.

The following ethnic groups and castes have been identified as the untouchables (many of these castes have been mentioned in 1853 civil code and subsequent publications have declared them officially as untouchables).

The following table helps to identify the spatial distribution of the population of ethnic and caste groups in Nepal:

	Caste/Ethnicity	Population	Percentage
Hill Dwellers	Kami (blacksmith)	963655	5.21
	Damai (tailor)	367989	2.11
	Sarki (cobbler)	276244	1.5
	Gaine (singer)	44484	0.24
	Badi (entertainer)	7082	0.04
Terai Dwellers	Chamar	203919	1.1
	Kalwar	162046	0.88
	Dushadh	93242	0.5
	Dhobi	76594	0.41
	Khatwe	66612	0.36
	Mushahar	141890	0.77
	Raji	19103	0.1
	Teli	250732	1.36
	Kushwa	205797	1.11
Total		**2879459**	**15.69**
The caste and	Satar (Santhal)	Sunar	
Population	Kisan	Hudke	
not mentioned	Darau	Dum	
	Kasai	Lohar	
	Kushle		
	Pode		
	Chyame		

Source: Statistical Pocket Book, CBS HMG, 1994

The table above clearly shows the castes missed out in the statistics, which count hundreds of thousands in number. Therefore, the population of Dalits can be estimated between 16-20% of the total national population. This, then, comes to be approximately 4.6 million out of 23 million population as of 2000.

The geographical distribution of Dalits is not uniform, particularly, the hill dwellers are scattered throughout Nepal whereas the Terai dwellers are concentrated in larger communities mostly in eastern and central part of the country. The hill Dalits are found to have settled either on the top of the hill/mountain or at the fringes of the settlement of the higher caste people.

Among the Dalits there is caste system and they have been divided into two. A caste called Teli from Terai, Kusle and Kasai from Kathmandu valley are untouchable but upon having physical contact by an upper caste he or she does not have to sprinkle water. The meat and milk touched and served by Kasai would not be considered impure. The rice offered by Kusle to sons of deceased during a mourning period is considered sacred. The Teli of Terai are considered untouchable but they are allowed to trade. Therefore, except Kusle two of these have been able to establish good business and from economic point of view they have already gained the higher status.

The Movement of Dalits

The society and state caused atrocities to Dalits for centuries but compared to the sufferings they had to go through, the struggle and movement are not so strong that challenged the society and state that would compel it to change the evil of untouchability and problems resulted by the caste discrimination. Therefore the situation of Nepal's Dalit still today has not remarkably changed a lot. Particularly on the economic front, most of the Dalits have become poorer than before. The movements of Dalit have been divided into four stages (1) Movements before 1950 (during the Rana regime) (2) Movements after the democracy of 1950, (3) Movements during Panchayat regime (1961-1990) and (4) Movements after the restoration of democracy (1990 onwards). All three stages before 1990 have been considered as 'then' and 1990 onwards 'now':

Then

The casteism was prevailing for centuries and Dalits were always looked down despite their contributions, as mentioned before, in the unification of Nepal during 1768-1775. However, movement against caste system is yet to have emerged.

King Rana Bahadur Shah, during his period, (1775 – 1806) opposed the caste system and tried to organise feast to feed all castes together as he was the follower of *Joshmani Santa Parampara* (one of the Hindu traditions). It was indeed a great step taken by the King for social change at that time but he was not accepted by his staffs and later on he was assassinated by his body guard so the effort of reform on caste system died along with him.

During the Rana regime, which lasted for 104 years in Nepal, Dalits were compelled to live a life very inferior to animals as they were denied the opportunity of education. The education was even banned for other castes of Nepal but there was a tradition of becoming literate for them. Especially Brahmin community had access to read Sanskrit and religious book so they knew its importance and went to Banaras (a holy Indian city in northern part) to acquire higher education. Their education, indeed, encouraged to initiate the movement against the Rana regime.

Despite such adverse situation, especially Bhagat Sarvajeet Bishwakarma of Baglung and his fellow Bhagat Laxmi Narayan Bishwakarma formed an association called *Sarbajan Sangh*. Sarvajeet Bishwakarma (1939 - 1947) challenged the orthodox Hindu rule of Rana by wearing sacred thread called *Janai* which is only worn by *Tagadhari* (Brahmin and Chhetri) claiming that his caste was higher than the Brahmin caste called Kumai (Royal Priest group). He called them Damai by showing a proof that thread and needle is required during their *Shraddha*, (a commemorative event for the deads). He was asked not to wear thread but he refused and was put into jail in Palpa. I think, he was the first and last person from Dalit to be jailed on the ground of opposing casteism.

To oppose caste system, Jaduveer Bishwakarma in the year 1946-1947, founded an organization called *Nepal Samaj Sudhar Sangh* in Dharan of eastern region. As barber refused to cut the hair of Dalits , he led a social movement against it. His movement compelled them to cut the hair of Dalits like other castes. From this, late Hira Lal Vishwakarma made his ground for politics and became the only minister of state from the Dalit community during Panchayat regime.

Another notable name of Dalit movement is Saharsha Nath Kapali in Kathmandu who established an organisation called *Samaj Sudhar Sangh*. In 1954, Pashupatinath temple entering movement was organised as Dalits are still denied to enter the temples though they claim themselves to be the Hindus. In that movement about 1100 Dalits participated and 750 were arrested by the government. About, 400 arrested were women. In 1955 Mrs. Mithai Devi Vishwakarma organised the Dalit women under *Pariganit Nari Sangh* which can be regarded as the first Dalit women organisation of Nepal so as she was the first Dalit woman leader.

In 1960, King Mahendra abolished the multiparty system and introduced Panchayat system. After three years of this system he introduced new civil code in place of the civil code of 1853. This new civil code equalised Dalits with other castes. The system was very much autocratic. Forming organization and leading the movement was almost banned, so not much can be seen since 1963 to 1979. However, an organization called *Nepal Rastriya Dalit Jana Bikas Parishad* was very active which tried to organize Dalits from different parts of the country. This organization was never registered in documents of the government which means it had no legal entity. However, the organization was in existence because its leader especially Hira Lal, T.R. Vishwakarma and Mohan Lal Kapali had good relationship with the royal palace, so, despite the fact that it had no legal entity, it was not banned. Most of the leaders who worked for this organization tried to be nominated by the king in Rastriaya Panchayat as a parliamentarian rather organizing and doing something for Dalits. Their major task was to please the members of the royal family and their staff, so, most of the leaders in the quest of power, including aforementioned, were kept on fighting with each other.

In 1979, there was a student movement and consequently then king Birendra declared referendum to choose either reformed non-party Panchayat system or multi party democratic system. During the interim period of 1979-81, the system was liberal and all outlawed political parties were semi-legal. Taking the advantage of that period an organisation called *Samaj Sewa Sangh* was established under the chairmanship of Shankar Vishwakarma. I was also one of the active members representing the students. This organisation did not organize any mass movement but started an intellectual forum, as all the members were educated. Two issues of magazine called *Pratinidhi* (Representative) were published. The reformed Panchayat system won with slight margin and Constitution Reform Commission was formed in which late Hira Lal Vishwakarma was one of the members, it was indeed a great honour to have a representation from Dalit. The *Samaj Sewa Sangh* presented its suggestions to the commission on behalf of Dalit stating that the practice of untouchability should be made punishable by law and there should be reservation in education and job for Dalits. Despite a Dalit being one of the members of the commission those suggestions were not taken into consideration. It shows Mr. Hira Lal was not appointed to raise the issue of Dalit but to serve the interest of the king as an extreme loyalist to him.

In 1987 an organisation named *Jatiya Bibhed Unmulan Manch* was formed under the chairmanship of Megh Bahadur Vishwakarma. It was indeed an organization started by young students. As the name suggests, it did not start any movement but tried to bring Dalit leaders of different ideology and groups into one forum and started a scholarship trust.

Now

After the restoration of multiparty democracy in 1990, the movement of Dalit came into fast track. In 1992, a national organization of Dalits emerged as a sister organization of Nepal Communist Party (United Marxist-Leninst) by merging the two organizations namely *Utpidit Jatiya Utthan Mancha* chaired by Golchhe Sarki (member of upper house of parliament 1992-1998 from UML) and another organization

Nepal Rastriya Dalit Jana Bikas Parishad. The newly formed organization was named *Nepal Uttpidit Dalit Jatiya Mukti Samaj* which was formed by the initiative of Padma Lal Vishwakarma, a university teacher. This organization, however, launched several movements against atrocities and discrimination against Dalit and until 1998 it remained synonymous with the Dalit movement of Nepal. The famous movements are as follows:

Incidents Related to Milk Selling

The milk touched by a Dalit is considered impure but if an upper caste person takes the milk with him to the collection centre that would not be considered impure which is very strange. In the year 1993, three notable incidents took place, one in Chitwan, another in Sindhupalchowk and the last in Syangja. In Chitwan, because of the pressure of the Dalit the collection depot agreed to accept the milk collected by Dalits whereas in Sindhupalchowk as there was no pressure many Dalits gave up livestock rearing for milk. The incident of Syangja received widespread attention. With the involvement of other human rights organisations like INSEC, (Informal Sector Service Center), CWIN (Concern for Child Workers in Nepal), INHURED ((International Institute for Human Rights, Environment and Development) a overwhelming demonstration of about 1000 people was organised. The mounting pressure of the people and human rights organisations the Chief District Officer's (CDO) office and Milk Scheme Office of Pokhara settled the issue by agreeing to buy the milk from all without discrimination.

Gorakhkali Temple Entering Movement

The Dalits of Nepal consider themselves Hindus and are equally devoted as upper caste people but their entrance to temple in most of the places of Nepal is denied. There is a temple of Gorakhnath in the premises of ancient palace of King Prithvi Narayan Shah where Dalits were denied to entrance and they had to stay outside to offer worship. Therefore, a programme of entering and worshipping was organised where thousands of Dalits gathered together in Magh 11, 2050 B.S. The caretaker officer Ganesh Bikram Shah gave in writing that untouchables have been prohibited. But later on the 7th of Falgun of the same year the movement was successful. However, later a wooden bar was placed to prohibit everyone from touching the idol. The positive aspect is that all are being treated eqally irrespective of their castes.

Shipapokhare Spring Water-scooping Struggle

In Nepal the purity and practice of untouchability is based on the acceptance or non-acceptance of water. The whole caste system has been divided into two categories. If one accepts water touched by another person, it is considered upper caste and if the touched water can't be accepted it is a lower caste or untouchables. Therefore, the practice of untouchabilty can be seen in public tap stands and spring sources. In Sipapokhare village of Sindhupalchowk district there is a settlement of Brahmin and Dalit who use the same source of water. The source used by Brahmin is better and water comes throughout the year whereas Dalits have to use the source below the spring where during the dry season they have to wait for a Brahmin person to come and pour water into the vessel of Dalit, On the 11th of Falgun 2050 B.S. a mass comprising Dalit and leaders of major political parties gathered in that place and scooped water. Prior to that incident a ten-year-old Dalit girl died near the spring source and it was suspected that a Brahmin woman had beaten her and pushed her into the water to death as the girl touched the vessel of the woman. Surprisingly, no action was carried out by police.

Bhotenamglang Incident

Ashadh 1st of 2056 B.S., in a teashop of Bhotenamlang VDC of Sindhupalchowk district, Ward chairman Bel Bahadur Sunar and his fellow villager Ishwar Sunar were beaten by the shopkeeper on the ground of making the shop impure. The ASI of police Indra Bahadur Tripathi put them in the custody. Later on another gentleman Indra Bahadur Gurung released them from the custody with a promise of paying Rs. 40,000. The news was published in the *Kantipur* daily on the front page, which caught the attention of Dalit activists and NGOs. Later the ASI of police was compelled to apologize. In this incident Dalit NGO played a significant role not only to overcome the problem but also to raise the awareness of general people through press conference and it was a note of cautions among police personnel not to repeat the same incident in other parts of the country.

Movement for Dalit Bill

For the first time in the history of Dalit movement, in 1998, the president of *Nepal Dalit Sangh*, Man Bahadur along with his fellow workers sat on hunger strike (against its own party Nepali Congress), in front of the party office. After two days of strike, the party agreed to make special provision for Dalits at all levels of party structure and bring a bill in favor of Dalits in the forthcoming parliament if it gets elected and forms government. The party was supposed to nominate candidates from Dalits community for parliamentary election but due to various reasons none of the Dalits was selected. According Mr. Vishwakarma, that event was organized to show the resentment and get something for Dalits. Consequently, such provisions were included in the election manifesto of Nepali Congress. Three years after the election, the government of Nepli Cogress brought the draft bill in the process with the committee under the Ministry of Local Development.

Chamar Movement of Siraha and Saptari

Analyzing the Dalit movements of Nepal, one can notice the domination of hill dwellers though almost 50% of the total Dalit population lives in Terai. The situation of Terai Dalit is much worse. Despite their worst economic, political and social conditions, no more serious efforts have been taken. However, since June 1999 a movement among the Terai Dalits probably for the first time in the history of Nepal emerged. Here it is worth quoting the leader of Dalits and the exploited of India Dr. Bhimroa Ambedkar who said, "if you make realize a slave is slave, then he will revolt". In the same way *Saraswati Community Development Forum* of Saptari an NGO had run REFLECT (Re-generated Frerian Literacy through Empowerment Community Technique) centers for one year or two in which Dalits participants had discussed the reasons of humiliations to them and found carcass throwing is one of them. They refused to throw such dead animals any more. Since they were very much united the upper caste people of Madhupatti and adjoining villages did not protest. That success was replicated by the Dalits living in Siraha district and they too refused to throw the dead cow of former minister Padam Narayan Chaudhari and all the upper caste people joined together and imposed economic blockade to the whole Chamar community. The situation went so extreme that telephone booth owned by a Dalit was burnt down by the upper caste extremists. The Dalits filed petition against Padam Narayan Chaudhary in the CDO office but the case could not be concluded. There were several visits of human rights groups and Dalit organizations and had high media coverage. The social justice committee took the side of Chamar whereas the minister Mr. Gopal Rai, who belongs to indigenous group, pressurized the CDO to dismiss the complaint. There was no amicable solution for both parties but after the movement economic and other blockades were lifted. The same movement eventually has been replicated in southern part of Saptari district where Dalits are living in worse situation than in northern part. Now this movement has not stopped rather gathering momentum.

Analysis

The movement of Nepali Dalits against the discrimination and social injustice is more than five decades old but not much has been achieved yet. There has never been a national movement covering larger population of the country at any given point of time. All the movements mentioned above are either incidental or sporadic. The Chamar Movement of Siraha and Saptari District can be considered as the largest Dalit movement in last five decades.

There is no possibility of uprooting the deep-seated crisis of casteism and untouchability unless there breaks up a strong uprising of large mass of people. Therefore I strongly advocate that the Dalits must bring a breakthrough to lead a strong movement against this stereotypical social system where prejudices and hierarchy between and among the castes formulates a value system. I even feel that it is not even legitimate to ask all the time for the favour from the government to make special provisions for Dalits. I still remember the tea party for Dalits hosted by then Prime Minister Girija Prasad Koirala where he stressed that the Dalit movement cannot go further unless the Dalits themselves come up with an urge to eradicate all the discriminations. He repeatedly said to the gathering, " I alone cannot do much for you unless you are united and enhance the movement yourself." If one of the strongest prime ministers of Nepal says he alone cannot do much, how can we expect from others. To some extent, I believe, he is correct because unless and until Dalits themselves and the organizations working for Dalits can create a sense of unity for the upliftment of Dalits, law and acts formulated by government alone cannot come in practice. Usually such provisions are misused by those who are in power as it happened with *'Upekshit Utpidit Dalit Bikas Samiti'.* About three years ago, this government committee, under Local Development Ministry, distributed Rs 1.8 million within two weeks to non-Dalits NGOs. As a matter of fact, the amount was targeted for Dalits to operate income-generating activities. This is one of the remarkable examples we can cite as total misuse of resources allocated for Dalits.

There are sister Dalit organizations of all major political parties of Nepal -- *'Nepal Dalit Sangh'* of Nepali Congress, *'Utpidit Jatiya Mukti Samaj'* of Communist Party of Nepal (United Marxist and Lenninist), *'Dalit Mukti Morcha'* of Communist Party of Nepal (Maoist) and so on. However, all these organizations are serving the interest of the political parties than the interest of general Dalits. It is usually said that they are forming vote banks for political parties in Dalit community but I don't think these vote banks are even being used as vote banks; their condition is much more deplorable. Usually in a vote bank system, something has to be done for the upliftment of the voters of the concerned community that comprises the bank. But in our case, during the general election certain political parties lure these voters by just offering *rakshi* (local liquor) and meat; as usual they are misled by the false commitment of those political parties. It would be injustice to see all Dalit organizations, affiliated to the political parties, with the same spectacles; some of them are sincerely working for the community as *'Nepal Dalit Sangh'* which is pressurizing to pass a bill in favour of Dalits. If this bill is enacted, it will be the greatest achievement for Dalits of Nepal.

After the restoration of multi party democracy in Nepal, NGOs of Dalit have emerged very prominently and it is very encouraging to note that the issues of Dalits have been taken more seriously by these NGOs than any other groups. Unfortunately there seems a lapse of continuing the spirit of the movement. For instance, right after 1990, for few years *'Utpidit Dalit Jatiya Mukti Samaj'* had almost become synonymous to Dalit Movement. However, lack of wide vision in the leadership spoilt the spirit of the movement initiated by this organization.

No matter, whether it is the incident of Bhotenamlang or Siraha, the beating incident of Kabhre or temple entering movement of Shaileswari Doti, there were the NGOs in those cases which not only took the issue but also compelled the concerned to take appropriate action against the exploiters as well. Particularly in the Chamar Movement of Saptari, they were the NGOs which played significant role and are still continuing the issue of filing public litigation in the Supreme Court to punish the culprit. Unfortunately neither *'Nepal Dalit Sangh'* of Nepali Congress nor *'Utpidit Jatiya Mukti Samaj'* of CPN-UML thought the necessity of releasing even a press statement. Interestingly, CPN UML, fearing that it will loose its voters by supporting the cause of Chamars, sent a warning letter to its active member Biswendra Paswan preventing him to involve in the Chamar Movement. As a result he was not picked up to be the member of upper house of parliament. Instead Mr. Rampreet Paswan of the same community who has less profile than that of Mr. Biswendra Paswan was elected and now he serves as vice chairman of the Upper House.

For last few years, NGOs in general seem doing better for Dalit than political and semi- political Dalit organisations of Nepal but it does not mean that the social justice- liberation of Dalits- can be achieved only by the efforts of NGOs. NGOs have certain limitations to get involved in the movement which is ultimately required to take a political turn. At the same time, it is very risky to be involved in the movement because there is a chance of being challenged by the non-Dalit community and even sometimes the government itself. Sometimes such movements can trigger a communal riot as it happened in Siraha.

Strategies for Dalit Movement in Nepal

Dalit NGOs are better organized and they have more access to the grass root people than the sister organizations of the political parties. The political parties and their sister Dalit organizations are not doing adequately for Dalits whereas the NGOs are serving them with various short and long term projects that deal with the real situation of Dalits. In such a crucial situation where democracy has not yet been institutionalized and people are still conservative, unity of people is indispensable. It not only gives strength to the discriminated but also helps to mitigate the problem. Therefore, all the NGOs working for the Dalits should organize Dalit people with all the awareness and start forming village level groups, federating them to district level and eventually at the national levels. A strong mass-based organization can initiate both political and social movements. I would like to cite an example of Parbat district where an NGO called *'Sustainable Livelihood Forum'* helped to form a CBO called *'Dalit Jana Samaj'* (Oppressed People's Society). Over ten years period of working in twenty-nine villages, it has enrolled more than 5000 Dalits as its members. They have been organizing different awareness programmes. The leader of this organization has emerged as a key figure and all the political parties want him to join. I strongly feel that all the NGOs working in Nepal for the Dalits or by the Dalits should take this as a role model and carry out the programmes. If the aforementioned propositions come true, there will be a strong political force of Dalits in Nepal which will be able to bargain any power blocks for their rights and justice.

References

Vishwakarma, Hira (1995), *Alternative Country Report for UN Convention on All Forms of Racial Discrimination, Dalit Sewa Sangh and Dalit Mahila Sangh*

Various Reports of ActionAid Nepal – Siraha Saptari Dalit movement

Koirala, Vidhyanath (1996), *Schooling and Dalits of Nepal: A Case Study of Bungkot Dalit Community.* Ph.D. Thesis, University of Alberta.

Legacy of Power, Politics of Image and the Formation of Dalits

Prabodh Mani Devkota

...The Negro is an animal, the Negro is bad...look a nigger!, its cold, the nigger is shivering because he is cold...the handsome little boy is trembling because he thinks that nigger is quivering with rage, the white little boy throws himself to his mother's arm and says-Mama, the nigger is going to eat up me!... I made up my mind to laugh myself to tears, but laughter had become impossible...

Frantz Fnon

This is the painful and bitter reality of a 'Negro'. May be a Black child who does not know what really the Negro is like, since it is the white man who terms the Negro. The word Negro is the colonial construct. May be today Europe wants to forget the past colonial history but Negro has remained as the powerful reminder of colonialism because time and again it gives us the image of a colonized person. The word never dies.

In our context too, Dalit is a term used by the non-Dalit community; it is the creation of the non Dalits. The term Dalit is widely used term in our context. Conventionally, the term Dalit is used to name the untouchable group though the meaning of the Dalit, as the Nepali dictionary shows, is the suppressed, exploited men/women or groups. Within such groups, too, there may be other suppressed castes and groups, which may not necessarily be the untouchable groups; it is a common term used to name the suppressed group. The very interesting thing is that the term has been used to address the untouchable groups like Kami, Damai, Mushar Dom etc.

Another interesting thing is that Dalits did not have access into the education system. The term Dalit is not coined by the Dalits, it is the product of the upper class people who possessed the education system, possessed the word power, formed the dictionary and used them.

The upper class group has created an image of Dalit who is unchanging, uneducated and untouchable. The formation of these images are the constructs of the imagination of the upper class people. This process of imagination is again the part of the power relation between Dalit and non Dalit community. Imagination can not go beyond the socio political, cultural and geographical boundaries, accordingly in this context, that tries to shape the identities of the Dalit community. Imagination is the dominant product of the existing dominating politics. As Edward Said says:

> *A second qualification is that ideas, cultures and histories can't seriously be understood or studied with out their force, or more precisely their configuration of power, also being studied. To be lived that the Orient was created - or, as I call it, Orientalized - and to believe that such things happen simply as a necessity of the imagination, is to be disingenuous. The relationship between Orient and Occident is a relationship of power, of domination, of varying degrees of a complex hegemony. (Orientalism 1995)*

Said finds that the relation of the Oriental and the Orientalist is based on the power relation, the relation of the

Dalit and non Dalit is also based on the power relation. Even in imagination this power politics plays a vital role.

Society is obviously based on the hierarchy; castisim is one of the major factors, which is the part of the socio-politics controlled by the upper class or the power holders.

Resistance as a matrix of power also exists in society but the dominant power incorporates resistances into the dominant ideology. They create the image which becomes an idelogy for the society and that governs the individuals like Louis Althusser says:

> *Ideology is the imaginary representation of the real world. What is represented in ideology is not the system of the real relations which govern the existence of individuals but the imaginary relations of those individuals to the real relations in which they live..." (Lenin and Philosophy 1971)*

In a society, people exist in an unequal power distribution. They belong to different cultural groups and the dominant ideology in different ways tries to control the public, which is the political project of the dominant groups. They try to invent the imaginary narratives, proverbs etc., which are directed by the controlling syndrome of the dominant groups. They create the "Others", "Dalits". Out of these narratives, proverbs, stories and abused words they aim to create the image. So they create an image, use them and control them. In fact the words create image and control the public psychology. When we name something, we are supposed to control the object, at the same time, we are controlled by the object. All this process creates the visual culture, which is controlled by the dominant groups because it is formed on the basis of who possess the power and who looses it.

In the Nepalese society, there is the extreme sense of castism. Dalits are regarded the lowest and untouchable castes. The upper class people from the centuries have developed the orientation like: "*aaphu mare doom raja*". (after my death who cares if there is the *Dom* king -low caste king) Raja or the King is regarded as the living God in the Hindu society and his place is replaced by the *Dom-Damai-Dalit*. There is the very negative connotation of the Dom. Upperclass people do not wish any positive image of the Dom.

In the Terai, when people denounce their enemy (even in upper class) then they say: "*Tan chamar, aaphulai khub thulo thanchas!*" (You Chamar! boasts of yourself?)Chamar belongs to the Dalit family. Here is also the negative connotation of the Dalit. He becomes the victim of the community. This process is the product of the power relation between suppressed and suppressor.

Another most important aspect of domination is the colonization of the female body in a hegemonic society. Female body is not only controlled in the physical sense but also controlled in terms of the land. Land which is regarded as the earth, the creater is the symbolic representation of the mother, this form of mother is also controlled by the male.

When people used to live in the primitive ages, there was no fixed settlement, in the geographical sense, land for them was a matter of God's gift. So, they never thought to possess it, it was always a sacred matter. But gradually along with the intervention of the politics in the human life, men started to fix themselves in certain territory. This process gradually led towards the concept of land owning system where it was the male who became the dominant one. This exposes the fact of the controlled destiny of the mass women in a patriarchal society. Among women, even the situation of the Dalit women is worst. Here I would like to associate the academic ideas with practical situaiton of the Dalits.

"Badis are untouchable Hindu caste with total population of approximately 17,000 who inhibit in scattered settlement in Salyan, Rolpa, Rukum, Dailekh, Kailali Jajarkot, Dang, Banke and Bardia districts of western Nepal. The history of the Badis is age old. In history Badi community used to serve by dancing, and singing at kings palaces and rich people or the feudal lords (Cox 1993) Badi females were used for the entertainment of the upper-class people. They exploited them not only in the form of art rather there was massive sexual exploitation. Out of this phenomenon prostitution started to take its speed and in the later days gradually started to shape it as a part of the culture. Generally these people do not have land and property. As a consequence their settlement gradually changed as the shelter for prostitution because prostitution was taken as a source of livelihood. Throughout the night people used to enjoy in the same settlement and in the day they denounced the place, the people and their settlement. The places are symbolically colonized, exploited as the body of the Badini (Female Badi). The society has created a visual image of Badini as the worst woman in all terms. So, whenever scolding to the girls even in upper class, people use the terms like: *Tan Badini!, Bessey! Randi!* (You Badi Women! prostitute! widow!) All these terms are used for Badinis to create the negative images. In this way society creates the situation, creates the image, uses them and exploits them.

Today, the places like *Kalakhola* (Dang) and *Gaganganja* (Banke), which were regarded as the shelters for prostitution, are in the process of leaving the old tradition. In Dang, there have been tremendous changes taking place, yet the image of Kalakhola that the society has created has remained untouched by the recent developments. We can say that gradually no Badini will be engaged in the sex work as a commercial sex worker, as they are described, but the social orientation and the image that the society has created will rule the public psyche. This is the politics of our tradition and culture. This politics emerged as the outcome of the real power relation between and among the oppressed and the oppressor. Through the power and politics the upper class people created the so-called truth that still tries to suppress the Dalits.

Accordingly, the myth of untouchability is the formation of the power. Whatever narratives and proverbs or the orientation that are created to dehumanize the Dalits have been taken as the truth. The upper class people formed the truth and distributed them. The tragedy of the marginalised people was that they also internalized the so-called truth which was formed by the power. They internalized the process because there was no way out of it.

Power is some thing that is exercised; it is exercised only when it is realized by certain group. Power does not occur in vacuum. Indeed power determines the structure of the society. No one can escape from the domain of power. At the same time all are in search of the will to power. Power is more than what is believed, power is more than what is felt. Power occurs; it happens and it dominates; it becomes a subject to be internalized.

Michel Foucault, the power analyst does not believe of power, as something possessed by those who exercise it. He believes power is exercised rather than possessed. Power is not property, or possession. Power is not simply what dominant class has and the oppressed do not. For Foucault power is a strategy and dominated are as much a part of the network of power relations and the particular social matrix as the dominating. So, Dalits are equally the parts of this power relation. Dalits are suppressed by the upperclass people but the tragedy is that within Dalit community the upperclass Dalit dominates the lower caste Dalit. There too exists the caste discrimination within the Dalit community. So in different ways Dalits are also the parts of the politics and the system of power. But the crucial thing is that the ideals of discrimination were developed by the upper class in the name of religion, law and culture, and Dalit community internalized the process which was institutionalized. This process and function of power should be critically analyzed within the Dalit community in order to create the integrated force of power of Dalit community. So that it can equally function with the dominating non-Dalit community in the matrix of power relation.

Power is not static, it has its own dynamics of changing. Dalit community needs to change the taboos of discrimination within the community to bring the change in their relation with the so-called untouchable group. Foucault says,

> *Each society has its regime of truth, its general politics of truth; that is the types of discourse which it accepts and makes functions as true; the mechanism and instances which enables one to distinguish true and false statements, the means by which*

each is sanctioned; the techniques and procedures accorded value in the acquisition of truth; the status of those who are charged with saying what counts as true (Foucault The Critical Reader 1986)

Dalit community should realise that the myth of untouchability as a part of truth was created by the politics of power imposed by the upper class. It is the power that creates the truth, so Dalit community can also create the truth (which they are insisting now), and their history. Decolonizing the colonized image of Dalits, seems the primary concern for Dalit movement. For this the voices should come out from the community. As much as possible Dalit community needs to occupy the places in politics, education, economy etc. It should be realized that no one can represent the Dalits, so self representation is essential. This bold and confidant self exploration will be the leading spectrum for destroying the colonized image imposed by the hegemonic society.

Works Cited

Althusser, Louis. 'Ideology & Ideological State apparatuses', *in Lenin and Philosophy & other essays*. New York: Monthly R.P. 1971.

Anderson, Bendict. *Imagined Communities*. London: Verso and New left, 1985.

Arnold, David & David Hardiman. ed. *Subaltern Studies*. VII. India: Oxford, 1996.

Barth, Fredric. *Ethnic Groups and Boundaries: The Social Orgination Of Culture Difference*. Boston: Little, Brown, 1969.

Cox, Thomas. *The Badi & Prostitution as a Social Norm Among an Untouchable Caste of West Nepal.* Kathmandu, 1993.

Fanon, Frantz. "The fact of Blackness". *The Post Colonial Studies Reader.* Ed. Bill Ascroft, Gareth Griffiths and Helen Tiffin

Hoy, David Couzens.Ed.*Foucault A Critical Reader.* London: Oxford,1986.

Rayamajhi, Sangita. *Who is the Daughter of Nepal?* Kathmandu: Across, 2001.

Said W. Edward, *Orientalism.* England: Penguin Books, 1995

Empirical Glimpses of the Situation of the Dalits in Nepal

Jit B. Gurung

Background

Despite the emergence of Dalit issue in the national arena in the recent years, efforts have been lacking both in the government and non-government sectors to attain a clear picture of the situation of the Dalit population of the country. It is so much so that today we do not even have a Dalit population figure, which is convincing in terms of methodology used to arrive at a figure. This situation is also a result of the lack of exercise involving the delineation of different Dalit groups. In 1998 the United Nation Development project in Nepal commissioned a study seeking to generate a comprehensive picture of the situation of the Nepali Dalits. The report came out in 1999. The author led this research endeavor. The study was conducted in 18 districts representing different physiographic regions. A multi-method strategy was involved. Nonetheless, household survey involving 5200 households was the most important of the methods used. The sample was drawn from four categories of households: a) Bahun-Chhetri; b) Ethnic groups (*jatis* or *janajatis*); c) Dalits (untouchables) and d) Groups that do not belong to the *Bahun--Chhetri*, Ethnic and Dalit categories (*Marwari, Yadav,* etc.). The findings in the following pages are organized in such a way that firstly sociocultural conclusions related to caste based ideologies, sentiments, perceptions and lifeworlds are presented. Secondly, conclusions regarding the economic and related manifestations of the caseist ideology on the Dalits are presented. (The generalizations are based on quantitative evidences)

Sociocultural Milieus

Casteism as Ideology

If ideology is taken as a set of ideas, beliefs and values about the way that the social world works, and by extension about the way the world ought to work, then we might expect the term to be fairly neutral. It may also be noted that initially the term also meant the "study of ideas", a study which was intended to be one of the great intellectual achievements of revolutionary France. Today Marxian discourse and even discourse outside it generally use the term with negative connotations: in such discourses ideology is considered illusory and erroneous, "false consciousness", and which is created and maintained to serve legitimacy to the relations of domination and systematically asymmetrical distribution of power between various groups in society. Marxian discourse, in particular, sees ideology as part of the "superstructure" generated by the economic "base" and which works to justify that base (which also includes the "relations of production") In these contexts the Nepali casteism is an ideology, in fact "dominant ideology" established and mobilized by the dominant classes (and thus dominant castes) to establish and maintain relations of domination with the lower classes (castes). The dominant ideology is mobilized in particular through what Louis Althusser calls the "Ideological State Apparatuses" or (ISAs) which includes schools, the family, legal systems, politics, arts and most importantly religion. The ISAs have been historically and contemporaneously active in maintaining the relation of domination in the Nepali society based on the ideology of caste hierarchy. Thus the traditional justification of ritual and status stratification which is analogous to the modern-day functionalist interpretation of the functionality of a system (caste system) is inherently conservative and status-quoist; casteism is an ideology because it is erroneous, "false" and legitimizes oppression, exploitation and domination.

Perceptions on the Origin of the Caste System

Higher proportions of higher caste categories tend to legitimize the existing caste system by giving it an aura of divine origin; both genuine personal beliefs and 'bad faith' to perpetuate the status quo act on the creation of this sentiment. More of the Dalits, however have come to realize that rather than God, man is responsible for the creation of the caste system.

Alienation

The Dalits are as alienated lot. Among the four caste/ethnic categories, the expressions of resentments against their own caste status is the highest among Dalit. The Dalits feel that the higher castes oppress, dominate and exploit them due to their lowest caste status. Self-alienation is not the only reality. The Dalit structure of their sentiment also indicates that they are also alienated from the larger society.

Fatalism

The proportion of the subscribers of the Karmic pre-determination of caste was found to be lower among the Dalits as compared to other categories. However, on the whole majority of the respondents believe on the pre-determination of one's caste. If caste is thus seen as a given, unalterable, fixed, the associated cultural and economic milieus also implicitly follow the same logic, clearing the ground for sociologist and anthropologists to argue for the existence of fatalistic worldviews and alienation in the populace. Karmic pre-determination is so strong ideology in the general population that the consequences for the Dalits are obvious. Nearly half of the respondents believe on the pre-determination of what happens in one's own life in this world. Although inter-caste/ethnic differences are not that much pronounced, the total proportion itself is important since how can a society advance if half of its members consider that the goings on in their lives are pre-determined? Even if the Dalits themselves do not see any positive functions of the caste stratification system, they still tend to express that to born into a higher caste family is a matter of "*bhagya*" (mostly interpreted as "luck").

Dealings

Treatments and dealings received by individuals are largely a function of one's caste/class status. Most of the Dalits believe that due to the hierarchical structure created in society they are considered inferior to the other caste/ethnic groups and hence receive bad dealings and treatments from their groups.

Status Quo

The caste Hindus and the Ethnic Groups (janajatis or nationalities) tend to support for the perpetuation of the status quo while the untouchables tend to think that the status quo is harmful to society. In this sense the caste Hindus and even the *Matwalis* are conservative socio-cultural formations-they tend to think that the caste system is functional for the society. No wonder today that even a traditionally non-caste ethnic group defines itself in terms of caste; the dominant ideology, or in this case the state ideology was clearly stated in the Country Code of 1854 by Junga Bahadur Rana.

Possibilities for Emancipation

Among all caste/ethnic categories, the proportion of the Dalits is the least in thinking that socio-economic advancement is possible within the prevailing caste system. As in most other similar comparisons the proportion of those seeing the possibility of socioeconomic advancement within the existing caste system is highest in the *Bahun-Chhetri* category. Other categories fall in between.

Prejudice and Discrimination

Prejudice towards and discrimination against the Dalits is day-by-day reality in Nepal. Prejudiced attitudes and discriminatory conducts on the part of the higher caste people are exhibited in activities ranging from interpersonal communication to civil society initiatives to the vast mechanisms of the state. A person's last name (which is a caste name) in a situation of interpersonal communication (whether dyadic, triadic or small group) can create symmetric / asymmetric, distorted / undistorted, and dominant / submissive pattern of communication based on who the interactants are in terms of caste status. Communication is one of the most important of human socio-cultural activities. More untouchables than any other group feel that they cannot communicate effectively in an inter-caste/ethnic interactional situation because of the inferiority complex developed in them due to the persistence of subjugation and domination and the consequent emergence of inferior self-definitions. It can thus be plainly seen that a 'culture of silence' in the Freirean sense, indeed prevails among the Dalits. Thus it is seen that there is a large population individuals from which are not able to 'talk' or to put forward their life situations in front of the mostly higher caste people who are supposed to uplift them from their current state of misery.

Despite some constitutional/legal efforts caste based prejudice and discrimination against the Dalits exist. Untouchability is still a pervasive socio-cultural phenomenon in the rural areas from which radiate non-commensal behaviors including restrictions on entry to temples, monasteries. Non-acceptance of water, and many food items, uneven access to resources, and segregated settlement. Prejudices born out of the concept of inborn superiority are also pervasive in bureaucratic behavior. If discrimination to some extent, can be outlawed by 'sensible' legislation and enforcement, prejudice is a state of mind, a psychological predisposition, conditioned over a long period of time and will take time for it to disappear even if anti-discrimination legislation are enacted and enforced.

Awareness of Development Interventions

Of all the caste/ethnic categories, the Dalits are the least informed and least aware of the existence of government institutions sent up for various purposes, ranging from the law and order related institutions to those that are directly related to development. They are also least aware of the functions and mandates of these institutions. Similarly they are also least informed about the activities of the non-governmental institutions. As a result the Dalits have the lowest utilization rate of the services of these institutions. On the whole, the reach of the activities of these institutions to these groups is comparatively very low.

Participation

If socio-economic development demands wider participation from all caste/ethnic groups in the affairs that concern them locally and nationally, political development in the framework of contemporary liberal democratic framework demands participation in the political process. However, political participation is highly linked to the caste/ethnic hierarchy. Thus more individuals in leadership positions at the national, district and the local levels are from the relatively affluent, higher caste/ethnic groups.

Findings pertaining to the socio-cultural milieus demonstrate that the caste hierarchy is not an abstract structure but a concrete system in the sense that even the four broad caste/ethnic categories considered in this study provide consistent hierarchies of manifestations in most of the situations examined. The Dalits occupy the bottom rung of the caste hierarchy, and they fare the worst in almost all the major comparative socio-cultural analyses performed.

Economic and Related Manifestations - Access to the Means of Production

Like in other agrarian societies land is not only the most important means of production, it is also an important determinant of status and prestige because it is the resource from which an overwhelmingly dominant portion of the population still scratches out its living.

The Dalit exhibit the least mean land ownership (ethnic groups and Dalits are the main cultivators of rented-in land). Thus in Nepal being a Dalit also means possession of less lands which means less household agricultural production and precarious household food situation. One may, in general conclude here that food sufficiency levels broadly correspond with caste/ethnic hierarchy and land ownership patterns. In this sense caste, class and productive capacities can be seen to be interlinked.

Unavailability of land for food production also means that involvement in off-farm wage labor activities is higher among the Dalits. Among all the caste/ethnic categories, migration for job search (mostly wage labor) is the highest in the Dalit. Although Dalits earn some income from traditional activities like tailoring, metal-works, shoe-making and singing, such activities are declining over time due to the availability of ready made garments, shoes, farm implements, etc. The Dalit group from the terai also has the highest debt burden among all caste/ethnic categories. Low landholding and consequent food deficits means that the Dalit burrow mostly for consumption purpose.

Household Income

The Dalits generate the lowest per capita income among all the caste/ethnic categories.

Expenditure Patterns

They have also the lowest per capita expenditure (due largely to low buying capacity) on items like clothing, medicine, and spices. Ghee, etc (modern amenities like telephones and vehicles and even bicycles are luxuries of extreme form which most Dalits cannot even think of). The Dalits also spend the least on education and have the lowest saving and investment rates. They spend relatively higher amounts in kerosene and fuel-wood largely due to the absence of or inability to afford electricity (the Dalits have the least number of electrified homes and the least number of TVs) and cooking gases (they also own the least number of biogas plants).

Dalit Dwellings

The general condition of the Dalits is also reflected in the types of houses they live in. Among all the caste/ethnic categories the Dalit houses are of the lowest quality in terms of the material used and forms and structures adopted. Most Dalit households lack separate kitchens with smoke-outlets; improved cooking stoves are not in widespread use and use of traditional *agenu* (fireplace) for cooking stall prevails. The state of cleanliness of the house and its environs is the worst among all the caste/ethnic categories due largely to the absence to separate cattle-sheds and waste disposal systems. Flush/pan and pit latrines are rare. Thus, on the whole the Dalit dwellings and are the most unhygienic among all the caste/ethnic categories.

Consumption Patterns

The consumption of the three major staples (rice, maize, wheat) and other items like milk and milk products, fruits, vegetables and meat is the lowest among the Dalits.

Health

In a situation where the per capita calories supply is far below the minimum required, the lower food intake situation, the unhygienic dwelling and sanitation practices of the Dalit communities are manifested in malnutrition, disease (incidence of diarrhea and pneumonia are higher among the Dalits than in any caste/ethnic category), morbidity and low labor productivity.

Population Structure

The population structure of the Dalits indicates that the dependency ratio is the highest among all the caste/ethnic categories considered. The burden to the household is high as both infant-population and child-women ratios are high in all physiographic regions. Early marriage is common in both the sexes but it is quite high among females. The Dalit group also has the highest early marriage rate.

School Enrolment

The school level enrolment is the lowest among the Dalits.

Biophysical Environment

Due to their unfavorable economic conditions and low levels of education Dalits exhibit lower environment consciousness. Dalit settlements and homesteads lack lush vegetation covers, and as a result are erosion and landslide prone. Not only is the extent of floral diversity conservation low among the Dalits, faunal diversity conservation is also low among the Dalits due to the absence, *inter alia,* of cultural restraints for the consumption of many animal and bird species.

On the whole, the economic condition of the Dalit today has remained stagnant as compared to other caste/ethnic categories. The Terai Dalits toady have the worst economic situation than the Dalits from other regions.

Finally to sum up, the cultural construction of caste/ethnic hierarchies have manifested themselves into similar broad hierarchies of socio-economic status of the people. In plain language, to born into a Dalits household means higher likely-hood of being poor and deprived (right from childhood to adult life), as compared to being into a higher caste household. Although the caste system is abolished legally the presence of the casteist ideology overwhelms all aspects of life. Privilege, opportunities, prestige, status on the one hand and material deprivation and deprivation of bases of self-respect on the other, are all linked to the caste-class nexus. Thus in virtually all aspects of access to socio-economic opportunities and subsequent improvement of life situations, the Dalits occupy the lowest rung of the ladder. This study shows that despite the presence of varieties of formal institutions (government and non-government) to uplift the socio-economic condition of the people, the non-formal institutions (most importantly caste, gender and associated patterned manifestations) have persistently acted against the Dalit's equal, uninhibited access to these institutions. Even if there are indications that the efforts of the non-government sector to uplift the Dalit in socio-economic terms fare somewhat better, here also the eloquent, confident, and relatively better educated high caste groups succeed in reaping benefits. Even if gender differences have been institutionalized among all the caste/ethnic categories in various degrees, the Dalit women have the worst situation in terms of gender relation vis-à-vis their men. Both caste and sex based prejudices and discriminations are rampant and the existing constitutional/legal provisions are largely ineffective in diluting these states of mind (prejudice as a product of the dominant ideology) and these practices (discrimination as result of prejudice) in a faster pace. All these milieus have acted on such a way that today poverty overwhelms the Dalits more than any caste/ethnic category considered in this study.

Hindu ideologies are obstacles to Nepal to Nepal's development plans, policies and practices.

Nepal lacks philosophies and systems of thought and discourse that can truly deconstruct these ideologies and demonstrate that these are indeed 'false'. Many archaic thought systems and practices have to be replaced by those that truly enable the Dalits and other disadvantaged groups to find their own ways to improve their life situations.

Refrences

Readers with interest on the quantitative aspects may refer to the main report: Gurung, J et al. 1999. The Conditions of the Dalits (Untouchables in Nepal: Assessment of Various Development Interventions, H~ ihar Bhawan, Lalitpur: TEAM Consult)

Social and Economic Conditions of Dalit Women[*]

Krishna B. Bhattachan

Introduction

There is a conspicuous dearth of literature on Dalit women. Many books, articles and reports on Nepalese women are published every year but none of these publications explains and analyzes the life and plight of Dalit women. It is not only the reports prepared by His Majesty's Government of Nepal but also by international donor agencies, including INGOs, grossly overlook the conditions and problems of Dalit women. Important government documents such as the "Concept Paper on Women's Development" prepared by the Ministry of Women and Social Welfare, "Preliminary Report on the Convention on the Elimination of All Forms of Discrimination Against Women" (CEDAW), "National Work Plan for Gender Equality and Women's Empowerment", "Beijing Plus Five Country Report" etc. do not mention any thing about Dalit women. These are indeed testimony of humiliation of Dalit women by His Majesty's Government of Nepal (HMG-N).

---

[*] This is a revised version of a paper presented in a national workshop on "Discrimination and Oppression Against Dalit Women: Problem and solution" organized by Feminist Dalit Organization in Kathmandu on March 7-8, 2000.

Also, it is a part of the continuing domination against the Dalits by the Brahmanist (or *Bahunbadi*) rulers. Inside such a dark tunnel there are some flashes of light-articles and books addressing the issues of Dalit women. Such flashes are indeed very encouraging.

When discussing social and economic conditions of Dalit women, one should not forget these four different sides:

- Both Dalit women and men are going through the similar conditions;
- Both Dalit and non-Dalit women are going through the similar conditions;
- Among the Dalits, Dalit women are discriminated and exploited not only by Dalit men but also by non-dalit women; and
- Among the Dalit, some Dalit women face specific problems.

I have divided this article into three parts: (1) social condition of Dalit women, (2) economic condition of Dalit women, and (3) main activities required to uplift social and economic condition of Dalit women.

Social Condition

Concerning social condition of Dalit women, I shall confine my analysis on population, crisis of identification, untouchability, social mobility, triple roles, sexual exploitation and trafficking, proselytization, use of mother tongues, victimization by the development industry and NGOs. Although, education, politics and health are parts of the social condition, I am not going to deal with these issues as these are addressed in other articles.

Population

According to the census of 1991, the total population of Dalit women is 1,147,933, that is, 12.3 percent of the total women's population of Nepal. Many Dalit intellectuals and activists believe that the total Dalit population should be about four million. Accordingly, the total population of Dalit women should be two million. Out of the twelve hundred thousand Dalit women, about a half of them are of the age group 15 to 54 and about five hundred thousands are less than 14 years of age.

The largest population of Dalit women is of the Kami with about five hundred thousand, Damai two hundred thousand and Sarki about one hundred fifty thousand (Table 1).

Table 1. Population of Dalit Women by Age Group

S. No.	Caste	Age Group				Total Dalit Women	Percent of Women's Total Population 9,270,123
		0-14	15-54	55+	Not Stated		
1.	Kami	215,480	244,471	31,587	79	491,617	5.3
2.	Damai	82,358	95,400	11,790	21	189,569	2.0
3.	Sarki	60,456	71,819	9,703	13	141,991	1.5
4.	Chamar	39,956	51,544	8,349	17	99,866	1.1
5.	Musahar	29,186	36,221	4,990	16	70,413	0.7
6.	Dusadh	17,925	23,724	3,690	11	*45,350	0.5
7.	Dhobi	15,070	19,015	2,929	8	37,022	0.4
8.	Kanu	14,002	17,075	2,554	14	33,645	0.4
9.	Khatbe	13,127	16,875	2,465	4	32,471	0.3
10.	Badi	1,642	1,911	133	1	3,687	0.04
11.	Gaine	983	1,165	153	1	2,302	0.02
	Total	490,185	579,220	78,343	185	1,147,933	12.3

Source: National census, 1991 (Based on Table 25).
Note: * Error in the Census figure: 45,310

Crisis of identification

Both Dalit women and men still continue facing an identity crisis. HMG-N has not yet listed different Dalit communities in the Nepal Gazette. If the government fail to recognize and identify the Dalit communities, it would be impossible for such communities to get programs, services, facilities and privileges from HMG-N.

There are conflicting information about the number of Dalit communities. For example, Shiva Sharma (2054) and Kamala Hemchuri (1999) have identified 11 and 14 Dalit communities respectively in the Census of 1991 published by the Central Bureau of Statistics (CBS). Shiva Sharma has identified Kami, Damai, Sarki, Chamar, Musahar, Dusadh, Dhobi, Kanu, Khatbe, Badi and Gaine as Dalits (Table 1). In Kamala Hemchuri's article it is not clear which other three Dalits are included in the 1991 Census.

The *Uppechhit, Utpidit ra Dalit Barga Utthan Bikas Samiti* (Ignored, Oppressed and Dalit Group's Upliftment Development Committee) formed in 1996 under the Ministry of Local Development has so far identified 23 different Dalit communities. These are: Lohar, Sunar, Kami, Damai, Kasai, Sarki, Badi, Gaine, Kusule, Kuche, Chyame, Chamar, Dhobi, Paswan, (Dusadh), Tatma, Batar, Khatbe, Musahar, Santhal, Sattar and Halkhor. Although the Committee has identified Sattar and Santhal as two different Dalit communities, they are indeed one community (they identify themselves as Santhal and outsiders refer them as Sattar) but another such committee called the National Committee for Development of Nationalities (NCDN) under the same Ministry has listed them as one of 61 indigenous nationalities of Nepal. The right to be in the list of Dalit or indigenous nationalities lie sole on the Santhal (Sattar) themselves.

According to an anthropologist A. W. Mcdonald (1998:282), the National Code of 1854 has listed eight (8) castes belonging to the third caste group, that is *Pani Nachalne tara Chhoiee Chhito Halnu Naparne*, in the fourfold caste hierarchy. These are: Musalman, Teli of Madhes, Kusule, Dhobi, Kullu, Mlecha and Shudra. The same Code has listed ten (10) castes belonging to the botom of the caste hierarchy, that is, *Pani Nachalne, Chhoiee Chito Halnu Parne* ("Untouchables"). These castes are: Sarki, Kami, Sunar, Chunara, Hudke, Damai, Gaine, Badibhand, Pode and Chyamkhalak.

The Informal Service Sector (INSEC), in its annual Human Rights Year Book 1993, has identified nine (9) different groups of Dalit castes (INSEC 1994:355-359). These are:

1. "The communities engaged in making ornaments, weapons, pottery and other labor skills" such as Kamis (Hill Iron-Smiths), Sunars (Gold-Smiths), Lohars (Madhesi Iron-Smiths), Vishwakarmas (V.K.), Sobh, Snehi and Nepali.

2. "The community Engaged in Sewing Cloth ard Playing Local Musical Instruments" such as Suchikar or Sujikar or Damai (Tailors).

3. "The Community in Leather Profession" such as Sarki, Charmakar and Mijhar (Cobblers).

4. "The Community of Singing Gypsies" such as Gaine or Gandarva.

5. "Badi Community."

6. "Kumal Community."

7. "The community involved in Laundry Profession: Dhobis" (Washerman).

8. "The Untouchables in the terai (Madhes)" such as "Aghori, Karori, Kichchak, Kisan, Koche, Khatwe, Gandarva (Muslims), Chamar/Mochi/Harijan, Chidimar, Guidhara, Jhangad (Urau/Uram), Jhangar (Kacchhuwa, Kharawa, Bakala, Bujira, Bekh, Lakada), Doom/Dom/Dhangar, Tatma, Tanti, Toori, Dusadh, Dhuniya (Muslim), Dhobi, Nat, Pamariya, Paswan, Pasi, Bantar, Bhilla, Bhuiya, Mirshikar, Munda, Musahar (Sada), Rachwar, Sharbanaga, Hahi (muslim), Satar, Santal (Satar), Halkhor, etc."

9. "The Untouchables within the Newar Community" such as Kasais (Butchers), Podes, Chyames and Napit (Barbers).

Among the castes listed as Dalits by INSEC, castes, namely Kumal, Kisan, Jhangad/Jhangar and Santhal/Satar are listed as nationalities by HMG-N.

Based on socio-cultural charactersitics, Dalits may be divided into three main groups: (1) Hill Dalits, (2) Madhesi Dalits, and (3) Newar Dalits. Both Hill Dalits and Madhesi Dalits belong to four-fold Hindu Varna model but Newar Dalits are the product of Hinduization of the Newars, who belong to one of 61 indigenous nationalities of Nepal, in the last six centuries (Bhattachan 2056). Damai, Kami, Sarki and Gaine are the main Hill Dalits. Similarly, Dusadh, Musahar, Chamar, Dom, Halkhor, Batar, Khatbe, Tatma and Badi are the main Madhesi Dalits. Kasi, Pode and Chyame are the main Newar Dalits. Mother tongues of Hill Dalits is Nepali and of Madhesi Dalits are Maithili, Bhojpuri and Awadhi. Newar Dalits' mother tongue is Nepal Bhasa.

Till now only three Dalit communities are organized at the national level. These are: Mijar Samaj, Biswakarma Samaj and Pariyar Samaj. Other Dalit castes have yet to get organized. Most of the Dalits are organized as Dalits either as fraternal or sister organizations of different political parties or as non-governmental organizations (NGOs). One such organization of Dalit women is Feminist Dalit Organization based in Kathmandu with its branch offices in different districts.

2. Untouchability

Untouchability is one of the hallmarks of Hindu society, culture and religion. One of the greatest crimes against humanity is the practice of untouchability. Hindus practice untouchability on two fronts: certain castes (Dalits) and women. Dalits are treated as untouchables round the year whereas Hindu women of both "high" and "low" castes are treated as untouchables temporarily during menstruation and child delivery. Both Dalit women and men are victims of the practice of untouchability.

The National Code of 1854 promulgated by Junga Bahadur Rana, founder of the autocratic Rana rule, reconstructed Nepalese social structure into four-fold caste hierarchy and placed the indigenous nationalities second in the hierarchy as the liquor drinking castes, though they never belonged to Hindu Varna model and caste hierarchy, and the Dalits at the bottom of the caste hierarchy. As the Code was the first ever law applicable all over the country, the practice of untouchability was universalized and Hinduized indigenous nationalities were forced to practice untouchability in every-day-life, otherwise they were punished accordingly. The New National Code of 1963 abolished untouchability legally but its practice has continued and unabated even a decade after the re-establishment of multi-party Parliamentary form of political system or democracy in Nepal.

Both Dalit women and men suffer from inhuman practice of untouchability. Dalits are prohibited or denied of certain acts and practices, access to common property resources, services and entry and participation in socio-cultural sphere at private, common and public places. For example, they are prohibited to fetch water from public water sources, enter restaurants, temples, shops, house, cowsheds etc, and participate in feasts. Furthermore, Milk Collection Centers refuse to buy milk brought by the Dalits. Also, Dalit women and men are compelled to engage in forced labor and they are discriminated in occupations, educational institutions, enjoying political rights, receiving government and donor supported programs. Many Dalit women and men face atrocities from "high castes." Dalit women get overburdened as they belong to the lowest rank in the caste hierarchy and also being women. Such practices are prevalent not only in the villages but also in towns, including the capital city Kathmandu. According to Kamala Hemchuri (1999:10), although all Dalits are equally humiliated and victimized by the "high castes" through the practice of untouchability, it is the women who suffer most. She mentions that Dalit women either have to wait for a long time to fetch water or are often beaten while fetching water from the public water sources.

The practice of untouchability is very severe in Madhes and the Hills of Mid-Western and Far-Western Development Regions. It is relatively less severe in urban areas. It is least practiced in the eastern parts of Nepal adjoining Darjeeling of India where untouchability is almost non-existent.

The leaders of Hindu fundamentalist organizations such the Biswa Hindu Mahasangh and Pashupati Sena never get tired of misleading people by falsely claiming equality and liberal humane values in Hindu religion and culture where untouchability does not exist. Which is nothing but a lie.

Padma Lal Biswakarma (2054:27) has mentioned that untouchability is practiced within the Dalit communities as well. For example, Kamis do not touch Sarkis, Sarkis do not touch Damais, Damais and Gaines do not touch Badis. Untouchability must be denounced whoever practices it. Dalits cannot and should not be an exception. It, however, should be noted here that Dalits practice untouchability among themselves as a demonstration effect of Hindu caste hierarchy.

During the period menstruation and child delivery, Hindu women of both "high" and "low" castes are treated as untouchables. The difference between "high" caste and Dalit women is that the former do not face any social abuse, though women in the hills of Far-Western and Mid-Western development regions, they have to stay in a hut locally known as "Chaupadi."

3. Social mobility

Compared to women of "high" castes, Dalit women apparently have relatively high social mobility. Their mobility, however, is due to their compulsion to get employment, including labor works. Their freedom to move outside the four walls of their houses is meaningless because neither Dalit women nor Dalit men have been able to hold key positions in politics, administration and other governmental and non-governmental organizations. On the contrary, "high" caste women are confined within the four walls and they are totally dependent on males from birth to death but still they have succeeded to hold some of such key positions.

Sociologists and anthropologists have pointed out the process of Sanskritization where "low" caste people adopt norms and values of "high" caste people to raise their social status. Like some indigenous nationalities, some Dalits hide their surnames or family names and caste by identifying themselves with those of the "high" castes. Such a process of social mobility is one of the fundamental features of internal colonization by the Brahmanbadis or Bahunbadis through the (mis) use of power and authority.

4. Triple roles

Dalit women, like any other Nepalese women, perform three roles: (1) reproductive, (2) productive, and (3) community. They spend most of their time in reproductive and domestic works, such as giving birth to babies, child care, cooking, washing clothes, fetching water and firewood and raising animals. They also work as a farm or agriculture laborers, daily wageworkers, traditional occupational works and household productions. They attend in social activities such as birth, marriage, death and festivals.

5. Sexual exploitation and trafficking

Dalit women along with women belonging to indigenous nationalities and Bahun-Chhetri castes have increasingly becoming victims of trafficking and sex work in Indian brothels. Many brokers and agents of trafficking of women sell women, including some Dalits, for few thousand rupees by attracting these innocent girls/women for employment, visit to cities and marriage ("false marriage").

Often "high caste" men pretend to fall in love with Dalit women and after having sexual relationship they either disappear or break their relationship. In few cases even if the "high" caste boy is serious and committed to marry with Dalit women, they live either in secret or become outcaste if the boy's parents or family members and relatives deny to recognize the marriage relationship. Children born from illicit relationship do not get family name of their father and eventually they would have problem in acquiring citizenship certificate and getting education. Kamala Hemchuri (1999:12) writes, "Caste based discrimination is meaningless as long as ["high" caste men] play with the bodies of Dalit women but it becomes very significant if they should recognize such women in the society." She has noted that Badi women are the worst victims of such practices.

Referring to problems of inter-caste marriage among the Dalits, Jibendra Dev Giri (2054:80) has pointed out that if a Damai marries to a Sarki or any Dalit to another Dalit who belongs to different caste they have problems to accept to such marriages. Such practices are not the creation of the Dalits but instead reflect another feature of internal colonization by the Bramanbadis or Bahunbadis.

6. Religious Conversion (Proselytization)

Brahmanism (Bahunism) and Hindu religion are primarily responsible for the past and present of the Dalits. Dalit liberation has been a myth due to the poison of Varna hierarchy and the concept of purity and pollution of castes and foods by sacred scriptures of Hindu religion and culture. Both Dalit women and men wonder why they have been discriminated so inhumanely by those who belong to the same religion, that is Hindu. Due to extreme and cruel caste-based discrimination in Hindu religion, many Dalit women and men have changed their religion to Christianity and Buddhism for their liberation. Those who have changed their religion generally do not face such problems. Many of them have received opportunities to get good education and jobs. For example some Dalit women work as nurses in hospitals and clinics run by Christian missionary.

Recently, Hindu caste hierarchy has poisoned Christian community in Nepal as well. The dominant caste groups, namely Bahun-Chhetris, occupy most of the high positions such as pastors. Some of these "high caste" Christians practice caste-based discrimination against Dalit Christians. Such practices may be seen in denial of entry inside the house to the Dalits and marriage relationship between "high caste" Christians and Dalit Christians. Similarly, those Dalits who have turned into Buddhism are also becoming victims of such discrimination.

7. Use of mother tongues

Problems related to mother tongue is a concern of two types of Dalits, Newar Dalit and Madhesi Dalits. It is not a problem of other Hill Dalits, such as Damai, Kami and Sarki because their mother tongue, like Bahun-Chhetris, is Khas Nepali language, the only official language of Nepal. The Newar Dalits such as Kasai, Chyame and Pode speak Nepal Bhasa (Newar language) and Madhesi Dalits such as Chamar, Musahar, Dusadh and Dom speak Maithil, Bhojpuri and Awadhi languages. Due to discriminatory language policy of the government many Dalit women and girl child are deprived of education, including basic and primary, and non-formal education. They are deprived of using their mother tongues in the government offices and schools. Lack of education has further deprived them from jobs and other opportunities.

8. Lack of Awareness

There is a lack of awareness among the Dalit women and men. They continue to become victims from Brahmanistic thoughts, policies and practices but they are not aware about it. According to Hisila Yami (2052:53), "Dalit women are suffering from three types of discrimination. On the one hand, they, being women, are exploited by patriarchy and being Dalit, on the other hand, they are exploited by the "high castes". Again, within the households, they suffer from their male family members. Thus Dalit women are living a life of more Dalit within their own community." If Dalit women would have been aware about such exploitations, they would have initiated strong movements and insurgencies.

9. Victimization by the Development Industry and NGOs

In Nepal donors open their wallets for women's empowerment (or gender issues) and poverty alleviation or reduction. Both development industry and NGOs claim to work for women and poor but in reality they sustain status quo. They indeed never reach out to the poorest of the poor, that is Dalit women. Whether it is the government or non-government, in both sectors high caste men and women reap the harvest. The development industry run by both the government and non-government is more project-oriented than movement-oriented. Democracy is the system that is of the people, to the people and by the people but in Nepal there are organizations which work to the or for the Dalit but they never give opportunity to the Dalits to work by themselves. Some smart Dalit women and men are co-opted by these "main-stream" governmental and non-governmental organizations killing the movement.

Dalit Women in Women's and Dalit Movement

The history of both women's and Dalit movements are five decades old. So far women's movement is dominated by women belonging to the dominant caste—Bahun-Chhetris and the Newars. Most of the Newar women who are front runners in the women's movement are mostly Hinduized. Most of the leaders of women's right movement do not like an idea of social, cultural and religious pluralism among women. Unfortunately, they wrongly believe that it is divisive and communal. Dalit women and women belonging to other minority groups hardly get any opportunity to hold key positions in such movements. Therefore, we see negligible presence of Dalit women in the activities and programs organized by the organizations leading women's movement.

Dalit movement is also gaining momentum. Although most of the leaders of the Dalit movement are Dalit men, nevertheless Dalit women leaders are also coming up. Dalit women are organized under the Feminist Dalit Organziation and Dalit NGO Federation with more than fifty affiliated Dalit NGOs is led by many Dalit women.

There is no doubt whatsoever that Dalit women can contribute significantly to both women's and Dalit movement in eliminating gender-based and caste-based discrimination respectively. Similarly, Dalit movement also needs strong support of the women's movement. Unfortunately, both movements are heading in two opposite directions concerning mutual help and cooperation.

Economic Condition

The overall economic condition of most of the Dalits is miserable. It is unfortunate that the Dalits who have traditional skills in sustaining agrarian economy live in poverty.

Feminization of Poverty and Dalitization

It is indeed true that there has been a feminization of poverty in Nepal. It is also true that there has been Dalitization of poverty in Nepal. Combined together Dalit women are at the bottom of poverty and socio-economic discrimination. Clearly they are the double victims of poverty, one as the women and the other as the Dalit. CARE-Nepal (1996:4) has identified the disadvantaged groups as those groups who are at the lowest social and economic positions, including illiteracy or low literacy. According to this definition, Dalits and indigenous people belong to the disadvantaged groups. If we add another criterion, that is women, in CARE-Nepal's definition of disadvantaged group, Dalit women remain at the bottom.

If we look at the economic and social indicators of Dalits provided by Dr. Shiva Sharma, it becomes clear that there is Dalitization of poverty within the Dalit community the gender proportion of economically active population is 85:101 (Table 2).

Table 2. Economic and Social Indicators of the Dalits

S. No.	Caste	Proprotion of Children and Women	Rate of Economic Activities	Proportion of Involvement in Non-Agriculture	Gender Proportion of Economically Active	Gender Proportion in literacy	Literacy Rate
1.	Kami	70.2	64.9	14.3	88.9	35.4	26.0
2.	Damai	60.5	64.8	27.5	87.0	42.5	28.0
3.	Sarki	a66.6	67.8	9.0	85.5	35.5	24.2
4.	Chamar	62.7	55.7	21.8	101.0	14.4	10.1
5.	Dusadh	62.8	53.4	23.8	100.0	17.9	9.9
6.	Musahar	64.9	65.5	29.7	99.0	25.0	4.2
	National Standard	61.6	56.6	16.6			

Source: Adapted from Table 4 prepared by Dr. Shiva Sharma (2054:117) based on the census of 1991.

Lack of Access to and Control Over Resources

Due to dominance of patriarchy originating from Hindu religious norms and values, most of the Nepalese women are deprived from access to and control over economic and other resources. Dalit women have access neither in private sphere nor in public sphere due to continuing practices of patriarchy and untouchability. Few Dalit women, as exceptions, may have some access to resources but they may not have any control over them.

Displacement from traditional occupation and lack of employment in both agriculture and non-agriculture sectors are common problems of Dalit women and men. Dr. Haribansha Jha (1999), an economist, has estimated that about 68 percent of Dalits live below the absolute poverty line and among the total Nepalese population who live below the absolute poverty line most of them are Dalits. In a country where Dalit men are suffering from the problem of unemployment it is difficult to imagine about employment of Dalit women.

There is no doubt whatsoever that Dalit women and men are rich in skills related to their traditional occupations. The processes of modernization or Westernization, urbanization, globalization and liberalization that have been unfolding in the last five decades have further marginalized knowledge, skills and products based on the Dalits' traditional occupations. Dr. Haribansha Jha (1999:4) has noted that the Hill Dalits, such as Kami, Damai, sarki and Gaine and Madhesi Dalits such as Tatma, Khatbe, Mushar and Dom have lost market of their traditional skills and products. Such processes of marginlization have pushed them to rely on agriculture or non-agriculture sector but there too they have no place for employment. In such a situation women become the hardest hit victims of poverty.

Table 3. Landowenrship of the Dalits

S. No.	Caste	Landless %	Less Than 5 Ropanies %	6-10 Ropanies %	11-20 Ropanies %	More than 21 Ropanies %	Total
1.	Kami	11.2	46.5	18.8	17.1	6.5	170
2.	Damai	28.8	55.1	11.5	3.2	1.3	156
3.	Sarki	7.6	47.8	24.2	16.7	3.8	157
4.	Badi	39.1	39.1	13.0	4.3	4.3	46
5.	Dhobi	33.3	66.7				3
6.	Doom	88.2	11.8				17
7.	Gaine	41.2	45.1	9.8	3.9		51
8.	Hudke	100.0					8
9.	Kasai	23.5	73.5	2.9			34
10.	Musahar	33.3	55.6		11.1		9
11.	Pode	21.7	56.5	21.7			23
	Average/Total	23.0	48.7	15.6	9.6	3.1	674

Source: Adapted from Table 18 in Sharma, Chetri and Rana (1994:43).

In Nepal, ownership of land means a lot in terms of wealth, power and social prestige. Lack of land means lack of wealth, power and prestige. For the middle and low class people, ownership of land means self-employment and non-ownership means unemployment. Data of Dalits' land ownership in Table 3 reveals that 23% are landless, 48.7% own less than 5 ropanies, 15.6% own 6 to 10 ropanies, 9.6% own 10 to 20 ropanies and 3.1% own more than 21 ropanies of land. If we mix up data of the Dalits and some selcted indigenous peoples as done by Shiva Sharma (1999:11), about 60% and if we analyze the data of the Dalits only then about 88% families are unable to make a living from their land. Thus they are forced to find employment in agriculture or non-agriculture sectors but employment in these sectors are simply not available. Lack of land ownership and denial of purchasing milk produced by Dalits by the dairy industries have made it impossible for the Dalits to engage in animal husbandry (Sharma 1999:12).

Activities Required for the Socio-Economic Upliftment of Dalit Women

To uplift the socio-economic condition of the Dalit women, His Majesty's Government of Nepal (HMG-N), donors, women's rights activists and Dalits should do the following activities:

1. HMG-N should identify the Dalits and list in the Nepal Gazette.
2. While preparing long-term and short-term plans and budgets Dalits should also be allowed to participate in the

decision making process. In the case of plan and programs for Dalit women, Dalit women also should be allowed to make decisions while preparing such plans and programs. The continuing practices of for or to the Dalit women and men should be abandoned.

3. All government documents should include issues and problems of and policies, strategies, and programs for the Dalits in general and Dalit women in particular.

4. Both HMG-N and all international donors, including multi-lateral, bi-lateral and INGOs should make sure that Dalits participate in the decision making process concerning planning, designing and implementing programs or projects. If Dalit organizations need capacity building, such programs should also be implemented.

5. Both HMG-N and the donors should accept the fact that the battle against poverty, illiteracy and socio-cultural discrimination cannot be fought if the plans and programs are not Dalit-centered. It must be realized that the development of Dalit women and men means the development of Nepal as well. Without their development, particularly of the Dalit women, development of Nepal would be a mirage.

6. HMG-N should formulate and implement positive discrimination of affirmative action for the Dalits in general and Dalit women in particular. Also, Dalit Women's department and Dalit Women's Cell should be established in the Ministry of Women, Child and Social Welfare, National Planning Commission and Ministries and Departments related to women, including Ministries of education, health, agriculture and forest.

7. Each Dalit caste should get organized at the national level and all such castes should be federated into a Dalit

Federation. All Dalit caste organizations should work together for the common causes and issues to fight against the continuing Brahmanism. Each Dalit caste should form its own women's organization.

8. Dalit women should claim and find their due space in the "main stream" women's movement. Also, Dalit women should be organized in such a way that they themselves should be able to launch a strong movement even at the streets. The "main stream" women's movement also think seriously to give due space to Dalit women without whose support women's movement would never achieve its mission and goals.

9. Dalit women (and also men) should form and alliance with other victims of Brahamanism (Bahunbad) and seek their help and support for their liberation. The most natural allies of the Dalits are indigenous people. In any case, Dalit movement should be intensified (Bhattachan 2056).

10. The human rights organizations and human rights activists of Nepal should take up the issue of untouchability and plight of the Dalits very seriously. Effective implementation of the Convention on All Forms of Discrimination Against Women (CEDAW) and the Convention Against All Forms of Racism and Racial Discrimination are important for the upliftment of Dalit women.

At the end

If women's movement in Nepal should succeed, it may solve part, not all, of the Dalit women's problems. Similarly, if Dalit movement should succeed, it may not solve the gender-based problems of Dalit women. Even if the Dalit women's common problems are solved, the regional or local problems of some Dalit women may not be solved. Therefore, there is a need for multi-pronged strategies to solve the problems of Dalit women. Dalit women should get organized at all levels and rely on themselves for their upliftment by fighting against the Brahmanistic norms and values and patriarchy. They should not continue to rely on others for their development. All the non-Dalits should accept the fact that without the development of Dalit women development of the whole country is simply not possible. If Dalit women march ahead in the road of development, the whole country would be marching ahead in the road of development. The sooner it happens,the better it would be.

References Cited

Bhattachan, Krishna B.

> 2056 "*Dalit Andolan Kina Charkanu Parcha?*" ("Why the Dalit Movement Should be Intensified?") Pp. 3-7. **Jijibisha**. Year 3,. Number 4. 2056 B.S. (Text in Nepali).

Biswakarma, Padmalal

> 2054 "*Dalit Samudayako Samajik, Arthik, Rajnaitik Sthiti ra Arakchyanko Sawal*" ("Social, Economic, Political Status of Dalit Community ,and the Question of Affirmative Action"). Pp. 20-43. In **Dalit Samudayaka Samasya Bisayek Rastriya Paramarsha Gosthi**. Kathmandu: GRINSO.2054 B.S. (Text in Nepali).

CARE-Nepal
   1996 CARE NEPAL Disadvantaged Group Strategy Paper. Kathmandu: CARE-Nepal.

Giri, Jibendradev
   2054 "*Dalit Samudayaka Saichhik Tatha Sanskritik Samsya ra Samadhanka Upayeharu*" ("Educational and Cultural Problems of the Dalit Community and Ways for Its Solutions"). Pp. 68-90. In *Dalit Samudayaka Samasya Bisayek Rastriya Paramarsha Gosthi*. Kathmandu: GRINSO.2054 B.S. (Text in Nepali).

Hemchuri, Kamala
   1999 "*Dalit Mahilaharuko Chunauti ra Sambhavanaharu*" ("Challenges of Dalit Women and the Possibilities"). A paper presented in a seminar on Democracy and Dalit: Problems of Untouchability in Nepal organized by the Centre for Economic and Technical Studies (CETS) in cooperation with Friedrich-Ebert-Stiftung (FES) in Kathmandu in June 4-5, 1999. (Text in Nepali).

Jha, Haribansha
   1999 "*Nepalma Teraika Dalitharu*" ("Dalits of the Nepal Terai"). A paper presented in a seminar on Democracy and Dalit: Problems of Untouchability in Nepal organized by the Centre for Economic and Technical Studies (CETS) in cooperation with Friedrich-Ebert-Stiftung (FES) in Kathmandu in June 4-5, 1999. (Text in Nepali).

INSEC
>   1994 "Highlight of the Year – Untouchables in Nepal." Pp. 349-379. In **Human Rights Year Book 1993**. Kathmandu: Informal Sector Service Centre (INSEC).

Sharma, Khagendra, Gyanu Chetri and Sita Rana
>   **1994 A Modest Study of the Current Socio-economic Situation of the Lowest Status Caste and Tribal Communities in Nepal**. Kathmandu: Save the Children US.

Sharma, Shiva
>   2054 "*Nepalma Dalit Jatiharuko Sankhya ra Arthik Samajik Sthiti*" ("Numbers and conomic Social Status of Dalit Castes in Nepal"). Pp. 112-121. In ***Dalit Samudayaka Samasya Bisayek Rastriya Paramarsha Gosthi***. Kathmandu: GRINSO.2054 B.S. (Text in Nepali).

Yemi, Hisila
>   2052 "*Rajniti ma Dalit Mahila*" ("Dalit Women in Politics"). In ***Mahila Utpidanbhitra Dalit Mahila***. Kathmandu: Feminist Dalit Organization. 2052 B.S. (Text in Nepali).

Education and Health Status of Dalit Women

Bidya Nath Koirala

Discriminatory Thoughts

Rigveda (10-90-12) legitimized structural functional frame of thinking. Different Vedas and Puranas (Hindu's religious texts) reiterated the structural functional paradigm. Saint Bhrigu (200 BC) legalized this functional paradigm and made it a social value. King Jayasthiti Malla, Ram Shah, and Jung Bahadur gave royal sanction and/or patronage to these social values through their "conservative reformative plan". The feudal ritualized this discriminatory culture and made a day-to-day business of the people. The education system reproduced these discriminatory practices (Bourdieu, 1976). Thus we continued our discriminatory mindset. We classified people under lower and higher caste groups. We reiterated the idea that Prakriti (nature) is inferior to Purush (spirit), women are inferior to men, Dalit is inferior to non-Dalit. Thus our discriminatory mindset got continuation in our action.

Why did not we reset our mind? Why did we continue the patriarchic notion? The notion that male is supreme, only male should hold property, only male has the right over women's body (Tuladhar, 2052 VS: 48). We continued the culture created by the "clever religion" (Aale Magar, 2052 VS: 48). Thus Dalit women were triply exploited: being women, being a victim of patriarchal society, and being women of the Dalit caste (Yami, 2052 VS: 48).

Reformatory Thoughts

Acker (1984 cited in Fagarlind and Shah, 1989: 168-169) categorized gender analysis approaches into two halves. The first halves comprise the fundamental thinking about gender. The second halves deal with functional thinking. Functionalist liberalism, Marxist feminism, and radical feminism come under the first category. These thinking analyze why the women are subordinate to men? The functionalist/liberalist women claim that it is the bodily structure that made women subordinate to men. So, only the consensus between men and women puts end of the discriminatory thinking. Marxist women claim differently. For them, it is class oppression, male as oppressor and female as oppressed. The power relation between male and female equates to the bourgeois and the proletariat. So women should be organized for the emancipation from male chauvinism. But the radical feminist in association with socialist feminists identifies two pressurizing elements. The first element is patriarchal notion and the second is the capitalist mindset. In order to get salvation, we have to change the socio-political structure.

The second set of feminists analyzed the social process. There they observed the production and the reproduction of masculinity and feminity: The production and reproduction of son being an attacking force and daughter as tolerating force. Home, school and culture were perpetuating the phenomenon of production and reproduction of masculinity and feminity.

Women Development Approaches

Vedic thinkers paid respect to women. They established the value that without woman man has no existence at all. But the Puranic (the interpreters of Veda and Upanishads into folk language) thinkers and the Smritikars (the scribers of the ancient mythologies) made an embodied culture to control women and Dalits. In their controlling frame, both the Dalits and women are the subjects to be penalized. Koran Sarif (24/31:216) and 24/59:219) and Bible (Old Testament and the writing in Bible after Jesus) confined women's sky. But some of the quotations of Bible (73:810; Timothi, 5:14 and chapters 7-9:820) gave some way out to expand the sky of women. Thus the "liberal thinking and the liberal interpretation" of the religious books suggested some women development measures.

The Western women of the modern world identified various approaches of women's emancipation. Moster (1995:151) classified those approaches as (a) welfare approach (b) equity approach (c) anti-poverty approach (d) efficiency approach (e) empowerment approach. The first approach targeted women and developed programs for them. The second approach devised policies and programs to bring women into the mainstream. The third approach promoted pro-women programs. The fourth approach developed women sensitization programs and led them to the mainstream. His fifth approach empowered, organized, and motivated women for their rights. But what the Nepali Dalit women achieved? They got skill development training from the welfare approach and some program from empowerment approach. But all the Dalit women could not get access to those programs. Only the women of the road corridor took benefit of the women's program. The rest of the Dalit women are leading the same life as it was a century ago.

Observable Changes Brought by Development

What the rural women got from the development? Dr. Meena Acharya (1997:11, 13-15) analyzed the available statistics and found that the marriage age has been raised by three years during three decades (1961–1991). More women are using family planning devices, more girls are attending schools, and the life expectancy rate is increasing. But the question arises – how about the situation of Dalit women? Team Consult (1999) studied the condition of Nepali Dalit. This study found that the condition of Dalit women could not improve in comparison with other groups of women.

- Only three percent of the primary school cycle completing girls of the Dalit community join in secondary school. The number of Dalit girls in higher education is negligible (P. 30).
- Only a handful number of Dalit girls join in primary school. This is a small number of Dalit girls in comparison with the girls of the other caste groups (P. 176).
- 46% of the Dalit girls from the hill, 43.4% of the mountain, and 30% girls of the southern plain, Terai dropout from the school (P. 32).
- The Dalit community has the lowest literacy rate (P. 176). And moreover, the Dalit women come to the bottom (CERID, 1997).

Educational Status of Dalit Women

	Mountain	Hill	Plain	Total
Primary level	17	27	15	20
Secondary level	3	8	4	6
Higher level	0	0	0	0

- Still 7.7% of the Dalit girls of the plain, 3.1% of the hill, and 3.4% of the mountain are forced to marry before they reach at 10 years of age (Team Consult, 1999: 27)
- Dalit women give birth more children than their non-Dalit counterparts (Ibid: 34)
- There is high mortality rate among the Dalit children (165 per thousand). Moreover many Dalit children are dying because of diarrhea and pneumonia. The mothers are suffering from virginal prolepses
- Less Dalit women are using contraceptive measures than that of the non-Dalit women (Ibid:36)
- Very few Dalit children are vaccinated (Ibid: 37 and 38).

Health Situation of the Dalit Women

- The life expectancy of the Dalit women is just 50 whereas it is 55 in non-Dalits (Mushahar's life expectancy is just 42 years).
- The under five mortality rate of the Dalit children is 109 per thousand.
- 50% Dalit children are under nurtured and hence they suffer from mal nutrition.
- Mother's death rate is 850 per thousand at the time of child birth.

(Source: Collection of Dalit Mahila Sangh, 2056 VS).

The above statistics indicated a single point. The point is: the status of Dalit women is weak. The efforts made by the government and non-government agencies are inadequate. So the Dalit movement has not been able to problematize the issue (Neupane, 2056 VS; Bhattachan, 2056 VS). What has been achieved covers a limited sky. What has been done is very little (Acharya, 1999).

Remedial Measures

Dalit women have observable problems. The first problem is how to take care of their children. Second, how to take care of their own. Third, how to ensure the schooling of their children. Fourth, how to be literate and continue the learning. Fifth, how to mobilize the resources around Six, how to eradicate caste and sex discrimination. Seven, how to integrate the on going Dalit movements that are seen in different parts of the country. All thinking demand solutions for these seven problems. The proposed programs are:

1. Know Ourselves and let Others Know

Where are we? What a nation says? What the development agencies tell us? Let us study and let others know them all. Message laden wall painting solves this problem. We can organize discussion session with local politicians and the community members. We can mobilize the teachers, youths, and students for such activities. We can share what we did with others.

2. Organize Dalit Women

Many a little makes a mickle. An organization is a most to consolidate the "little". Each village should have an organization of that little. These organizations fight against untouchability at the water taps. They can monitor the progress of their children in the village. They can motivate the DDC, VDC leaders to be Dalit friendly. They can emerge as pressure group. They can be motivators for inspiring parents to send their children in school. In all there may be many Dalit women's organizations. And they can work separately and/or initiate collaborative undertakings.

3. Sanskritize Dalit settlement

There is no culture for better health and education in the Dalit settlement. Let us lead movement to sanskritize the Dalit settlement. Let us change the living culture and eating culture, hygiene culture, speaking culture and other cultures.

Apart from the above solutions, let us go for specific solutions. The possible solutions would be:

(i) Ensure Reciprocal Training on Health

There are some minor health problems. These problems can be solved with simple understanding. The reciprocal training helps to resolve those problems. The positive deviance program of CBED in Dadeldhura and Baitadi would be a way of reciprocal learning in the field of health and hygiene.

(ii) Create Schooling Culture for the Children

We can see the school going Dalit children around mango trees. School does not pay attention to it. All the Dalit children are not schooled. There is a need of women awareness program, which help Dalit women to encourage their children to send them in school. We can pressurize others to send their children in school. We can prepare pro-

Dalit teacher in school. We can make the school as pro Dalit School. We have to organize discussion forums for the creation of schooling culture in the Dalit community. This changed culture will identify further programs.

(iii) Use the Government Policy

There are district education plans in all districts. Many of the districts have planned to implement compulsory schooling programs in the Dalit settlements. The High-level education committee (2055 VS) has reiterated the idea of district education plans. So let us use the government policy towards Dalit. In order to do so, let us activate the potentialities of the Village Development Committee and the resource centers of the school cluster program. Use the school outreach program and the flexible school hour program of the government.

(iv) Be Literate and Help Others to be Literate

We do not have to wait for six months to be literate. Even six days are enough to be literate. May be we can run full day literacy center for a week. This alternative approach helps us to be literate and make others literate. Non-formal Education Center of the Basic and Primary Education Program has piloted this concept already. We can do the best use of this idea to make the Dalit settlement literate. Conceptually, there is open learning program in the country. This idea can be capitalized to ensure post literacy and continuing education support for the neo-literate people. CERID in collaboration with Save the Children US has tested the correspondence post literacy and continuing education programs. Apart from this, Plan International has been thinking to run open school program in association with the local high schools. Let us use the learning of these innovative programs for the benefit of the Dalit community.

(v) Use Our Own Resources

The ruling politicians, bureaucrats, and academicians are being dependent in the international market. But the village people are not begging that way. There is skill in the village. And there exists labor exchange program. This system is everywhere in the country. The Dalit settlement also deserves these qualities. Let us give our hands and let us take their hands. Let us go to the teacher's home for labor exchange and ask teachers to teach Dalit children. So do we with doctor and ensure regular health check-up through DOT system. The same process applies with other groups of people.

Apart from the above suggestions, let us create hope among Dalit women: the hope that we can do something all by ourselves. This self-confidence ensured success to the Chipko movement in India and political leaders as well as social activists in the world. Let us devote ourselves for change. Let us go for picketing in front of the door of school and make the teachers and students pro-Dalit. Let us go for picketing in front of the door of the health post and hospital to guarantee health insurance of the Dalit community. Let us go for picketing in the door of the VDC and municipality and ensure development programs in the Dalit settlement. Let us block the door of the political parties and run Dalit empowerment and non-Dalit sensitization programs. Let us compel NGOs and INGOs to initiate development activities in the Dalit settlements. Let us go for home-to-home picketing for the elimination of gender disparity from each household. Let us go to the houses of the priests and non-

Dalits for picketing and ask for the elimination of untouchability. If we do so, we can improve the health and educational status of Dalit women. Otherwise, we consume our days to be old for nothing. Our children will reproduce us unquestioningly.

References

Achrya, Meena (1997). *Gender equity and empowerment of Women.* Kathmandu, UNFPA.

Action Aid Nepal (1997) *Situation analysis of the Dalit of Nepal.* A study of 6 VDCs of Navalparasi. *The Koren* translated by N.J. Dawood.London, Alhen Lane (1978).

CERID (1997) *Social assessment of educationally disadvantaged.* A study conducted for BPEP, Kathmandu: Author.

Fagerland, I. and Shah, L. *Education and National Development: A Comparative prospective.* NewYork: Pergamon Press.

Holy Bible by the Gideons.The Gideons International in Canada (1898).

Jha, Hari Bansha (1998). *Terai Delit:A case study of selected VDC of Saptari District.* Kathmandu, AAN.

Koirala, Bidya Nath (1996).*Schooling and Dalit of Nepal.* Ph.D.thyesis Alberta, Canada University of Alberta.

Moster, C. (1995). *Genderplanning and development: Theory, Practice and training.* London and New York, Routledge.

Team Consult (1999). *The condition of Dalit (Untouchables) in Nepal: Assement of the impact of various development interventions.*Kathmandu Nepal.

Legal and Political Position of Dalit Women in Nepal

Yubraj Sangraula

This article is an attempt to reveal different aspects of the problems that the Dalit women are facing. A sociological approach is employed to examine the factors involved in the problem. This article reflects my views and opinions rather than presenting any investigative findings.

Introduction

Each society has its own typical values on which its structure is constituted. These values play vital role in shaping the pattern of the social life. It is possible that great deals of such values are exploitative, and as such often tend to impose disadvantageous conditions on weaker sections of the population. However, the change in the paradigm of social value system is inevitable process of the social development. We find in many societies that the traditional hierarchical values have been modified by modernity. If we critically observe the social development process, we can perceivably see that it has always marched from tyrannical condition to the democratic setting with liberal attitudes. The worst form of tyranny experienced in the history is the "feudalism", which possesses the following basic characteristics:

- Power, signifying the status of person as a basis of the identity essentially based on the hierarchical structure,

- Aristocracy, signifying a societal hierarchy of the group with absolute grip in the resources with the help of political power, which in turn strengthens autocracy- it revolves as a circle,

- Occupation, signifying subjection or subordination of certain group under other group holding societal hierarchy. The subordination is effectively used to minimize the status of larger number of people who provide essential service to society- the group maintaining hierarchy claims absolute control over occupation.

The minimization of occupation is consistently used to undermine the social status of people involved in the given occupation, and as such has been taken as an effective instrument to hold control over them in suppressive manner. Many rules are founded in this course to strengthen the control of elite group, which in course of time are interpreted as social values. These values are then interpreted as the basis of societal governance based on caste and race. These values are therefore used as instruments of reinforcing the control of elite class to working classes. This vicious circle is an instrument, which operates to prolong the hierarchical (feudal) society.

In this way, feudalism indirectly gives the shape to the division of a society based on castes. The occupation is then defined essentially associated with caste, a prelude to caste system. A particular occupation is first designated to be carried out by a specified group of people, and the subordination of the group is then imposed on the basis of occupation. It means that Dalit situation is the offshoots of feudalism. Since, the leadership of feudalism lies in the ruling echelon of Chettris and Bahuns, the Dalit community is the victim of feudalism controlled by them. Historically, Bahun may not be politically aristocratic community as Chettris are predominant in politico-military power of the Nepalese society, however, Bahuns have maintained a huge participation in the politics of the society, and have constituted an essential element of the feudalism. Spiritually, Bahun community is the dominant class in the Nepalese society, and is the founder of so many anti-people values. In a conservative society like Nepal, by maintaining spiritual control the community of Bahun wields the local power most effectively. Hence, both the Bahun and Chettris are equally responsible to suppress the Dalit community. The division of the society on the basis of sex is another characteristic of the Nepalese society. The value system that segregates the society on the basis of caste is equally effective for division of the society on the basis of sex. Consequently, Dalit males are equally aggressive to suppress the Dalit women as in the Bahun and Chettri communities.

Problem of Dalit Women

The problem of Dalit women is therefore an offshoot of sex discrimination as well as the caste discrimination. Therefore, before going into critical discussion of the problem, it may be justifiable to begin with clarifying its characteristics:

1. The problem of Dalit women in broader context is a problem of feudal practice of the Nepalese society. Like their non-Dalit counterparts, Dalit women are abjectly suppressed by the values of the hierarchical society. Dalit

women's personality counts nothing for Bahun and Chettris. Hence, they are extremely vulnerable to the exploitation of these communities. Hence, the problem of Dalit women is a problem of caste distinction.

2. Since the Dalits have been the subject of suppression and exploitation in hierarchical social system, a major part of Dalit women's problem is an outcome of the exploitative feudal system.

3. The feeling of caste superiority is pervasive among Bahun and Chettri women. The upper caste women also suppress Dalit women. Therefore, the problem of Dalit women is a problem of social discrimination of women by women.

4. Each family has its own culture, values and characteristics. The superstition and conservatism take birth from the womb of tradition and lack of adequate knowledge and development opportunities. Such menaces are kept as vogue in the society. Dalit society is also largely influenced by defective culture based on orthodox Hinduism. As a matter of fact, Dalit males like Bahun and Chettri are equally suppressive to women. Therefore, the problem of Dalit women is the problem of gender discrimination within their own community.

Social Factors Behind Dalit Problem and Women

As mentioned earlier, the Dalit problem is a result of the feudal hierarchical system based on orthodox Hindu traditions. Religion often plays decisive role in shaping the culture and traditions. The problem of untouchability amounting to social hatred of certain communities, is a result of the traditions and cultures based on orthodox Hindu religion. The problem of Dalit women is therefore not independent of the problem of Dalit in general. Hence, at the outset, the Dalit women's problem should be analyzed in general and in connection with the problem of the community at large. It is an established fact that the community of Dalit is economically deprived and socially oppressed, resulting in denial of access to resources, development and education. It is indeed a fact that, therefore, the complete destruction of the so-called societal structure, which recognizes the caste based identity of persons, is the ultimate way to do away with all the problems associated with Dalit community. The liberation of Dalit women is therefore dependent on liberation of Dalit community at large. But the problem of Dalit women is not exhaustive with liberation of Dalit community itself. The liberation of Dalit community may liberate Dalit women from hierarchical societal suppression, but the gender discrimination within their own community would still continue. Nevertheless, the liberation of Dalit community will bring at least a guarantee of educational development for Dalit women as that of men.

Legally, the Dalit community has been freed from imposed values of Hinduized societal structure. New Muluki Ain (The Code of the Laws of Land) promulgated in 2020 BS. has prohibited the discriminatory treatment against Dalit community. But the execution is a complete fiasco. The main reasons for the failure of law to give effect to the change in the situation are multiple, but the disinclination to raise socio-economic and political upliftment of Dalit community is the fundamental one. The ruling segment of the society, which comprises a few Chettri, and Bahun and Newar families, indiscreetly neglected the fact that no liberation of Dalit community was possible without its soco-economic and political empowerment. It can be concluded that the lack of the political will of the ruling segment of the Nepalese society is also equally responsible for the continuation of the degraded state of Dalit community.

The constitution of the Kingdom of Nepal has guaranteed the right to equality, unequivocally prohibiting the caste - based discrimination. Indeed, this has succeeded to generate a popular basis for emancipation of the community. However, the provision is doomed to be stagnated, because the government has failed to introduce legislative instruments enforcing the spirit of constitution. Undoubtedly, the equality guaranteed in the constitution is therefore largely defunct notion. Equality requires competition, and competition is possible only among equals. The constitution guarantees equality, but the State has failed to address the longstanding problems of Dalit community. It means that State has forced Dalit community with all obstacles and hurdles to compete with community, which has enjoyed all privileges over the centuries. By instituting a system for open competition has set Dalit community to compete with groups which are socially, economically and politically advanced in development. Therefore, the state is not serious towards the wide spread problem of cruel inequality imposed on Dalit people. Only guaranteeing a set of civil and political rights can't be sufficient to socio-economic and political mainstreaming of the Dalit community. It can be therefore argued that the government must urgently enact a consolidated legislation to set the Dalit liberation in motion. Such legislation has to concentrate on the following issues for addressing the problem realistically:

- Provisions for special welfare package for facilitating the socio-economic and political development of Dalit community.
- Special reservations in matters of decision making in the issues concerned with their development interests.
- Secularization of the state bureaucracy with stiffer penalty for those who directly or indirectly involve in differential treatment to Dalit community.
- Sensitization of bureaucracy on need of elimination of differential treatment to Dalit, and
- punishment for violence, including sexual violence, based on caste basis.

Obviously, it is not fully possible to address the problem of Dalit women without addressing the problem of liberation of the Dalit community at large. To speak in other words, the problem of Dalit women is not simply a problem of gender discrimination. It is entwined with caste discrimination, and as such is a complex socio-economic and political problem.

Sexual Exploitation

Sexual exploitation of women is often entangled with socio-cultural milieus. The Nepali society, having based on the concept of women's inferiority, hardly recognizes the sexual exploitation of women as a problem. In a society which is divided into caste basis, the following two characteristics are obvious:

Sexual exploitation is rampant in the Nepalese cultural milieu, like rape, polygamy, incest, child marriage, forced pregnancy, multiple pregnancies, etc. These exploitations do not only

derogate the right to independent personality and life, but also cause a series of mental and physical torture, depression and social ostrasization.
For Dalit women the situation is worst. Many of such exploitation against Dalit women are simply taken as insignificant. Sexual harassment and assaults against Dalit women by men of so-called upper class are often in cognizable.

Sexual affliction on Dalit women is often ignored by the law enforcement agencies. It is viewed that " there is no question of chastity" in their case as the sexual affliction on them does not affect their social position. The sexual crime in Nepal is defined not in terms of violation of right to integrity of body, but in terms of violation of moral value. The existing value system maintains safeguard for protection of chastity of women, the violation which is taken as an invasion of the men's position or dignity in the society. This notion of sexual offence against women is a characteristic feature of the patriarchy and feudal domination. The sexual assault against Dalit women is therefore, by so-called superior castes, not considered as crimes against individual. The sexual violence against Dalit women is thus indirectly permitted under the existing societal structure of the Nepalese society, which is a matter of great shame. To observe at micro level, the so-called aristocratic Nepalese society is not ready to accept, or define, a sexual affliction on Dalit women as a crime in itself. This is obvious from having no law that prohibits or punishes a crime of sexual exploitation, which is merely induced by caste discrimination. It is also evident from increasing number of Dalit girls being smuggled into sex market. This development is simply a prolongation of practices of engaging women of certain Dalit communities for sexual pleasure. Girls from Gainee and Badi are the examples.

The following instances of discrimination further deteriorate the condition of Dalit women:

1. Women in Nepal, irrespective of their caste, are deprived of contractual, property and individual identity rights. Like their sisters from other communities, their sex and material status, i.e. they are not entitled to share in parental property, determine the personality of the Dalit women. The marriage is indispensable for them, and they are the husbands who are real master of their lives.
2. Like women in other communities, the identification of the children of the Dalit women is determined by their fathers' ancestral lineage. The children's nationality is not determined by mother, but by father.
3. Like women in general, a Dalit woman is subjected to a series of domestic violence and sex - based discriminations. The husband is entitled to consummate another marriage, provided that the first wife is not capable of having a baby within a period of ten years after marriage.
4. Family is composed after the father, the mother and sons being the subordinate members. Daughters are excluded from the family. The birth has been taken a qualification of the family membership for son. But daughters are prevented from having membership of the family by birth; rather the marriage is imposed on them as a qualification of the membership of the filial family.

Existing Nepalese legal system neglects daughters as member of natal family. There are two conditions imposed on her for getting family membership:

- She must remain unmarried, and
- She must attain an age of 35 years.

There has been no exception to these conditions. The natal family has only two obligations to daughters: support for subsistence, and giving away for marriage when she reaches 16 years of age. This condition results in:

- Deprivation of the freedom of choice, including the matters of marriage,
- Prevalence of child marriage
- Role of women is confined to begetting children for continuation of the family lineage of husband,
- Deprivation of the right development,
- Sexual exploitation of women and girls, including trafficking for sexual exploitation, etc.

Personality and Its Attributions

A personality is an aggregate of rights and duties recognized and protected by the law. However, a few rights are inherent. They inhere on people as inalienable rights. Rights which constitute the personality of people, can be grouped in three categories:

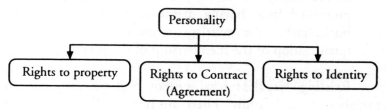

Every individual has his/her own identity. Nepalese legal system is absolutely silent in giving this right to women. For example, mother can't transfer her nationality to children as the citizenship of a person in Nepal. The father's identity is essential for the determination of children's nationality. Generally, it has been taken as a defect in legal capacity of child, but it is not true. Rather it is incompetence imposed by law on personality of women. Women have to always live under the direction and protection of men. Before marriage, she comes under the protection of father and after marriage she comes under the protection of husband. After the death of husband, she comes under the protection of son.

Rights to contract denote to the self - decision-making right. Right to property means the right regarding the acquisition; enjoyment and disposal of resources. The enjoyment of these rights largely depends on the dependence of the individual's identity. Deprivation of the right to self - identity automatically stigmatizes the other rights. Women's identity is always attached to that of father, husband or son. Lacking of independent personal identity negates the rights to contract and property. Existing debate of women's property right is not concerned with this aspect; hence the crux of independence of women is not addressed.

Legal Defects to be removed

Existing legal system has not only disqualified women to have share in *Aungsbanda* of ancestral property, but also deprived them of the right to self -determination. Therefore, it's not simply a question of discrimination on property right, but it is also a question of discrimination in personality on the basis of sex. It is clearly established that women's legal position in Nepal is defined in terms of their sex and marital status. Hence, the improvement of the condition of women means removal of all those instruments, which subject women under the control of men. The amendment of property right law does not suffice to the end. Removal of all discriminatory laws and enactment of affirmative laws should go simultaneously.

- The discrimination on the basis of birth imposed by the law of Nepal should be terminated. No discrimination based on sex should be allowed to prevail in matters. The existing law that excludes daughter from *Aungsabanda* must be terminated without excuse of any kind.

- The boundary of male dominance should be abolished even after marriage. Otherwise, woman will again be dependent on rights to be obtained through marriage. Marriage should be deemed as a result of an agreement between couples, and should not be viewed as a sacred relation to put women under the domination of men. Women should not be considered as an instrument of continuing the genetic lineage of the men. Hence, the following suggestions must be taken into account while thinking of independent status of women:

- Marriage is an agreement of consent, and as such it is a social contract. It can be created and terminated by consent. When spouses find accommodative to each other, they are bound by certain family obligations and as such both have certain requirements to behave in order to maintain the good relations. When it does not work smoothly , it should not jeopardize the life of one of the partners.

- Since empowered woman is a keystone of family, state should empower them through various affirmative actions. Hence, the special law, a complete bill of rights covering all aspects of life, should be enacted with a view to end discrimination against women.
- The laws which are inconsistent with independent status of women should be removed. The movement of women's independence should not be confined to achieve only the rights to ancestral property, rather it should be wider and targeted to achieve only the equal status of personality.

The constitution of the Kingdom of Nepal 1990 has guaranteed right against discrimination based on any ground, including sex. It's an established fact. No one can refuse this comply with this factual truth. The famous jurist of Hindu jurisprudence, *Jimutabhan* promulgated a rule of interpretation. This rule empowers judges to interpret laws in the way that the fact is established is unavoidable. (Factum Valet)

He says," Even hundreds scriptures cannot change the established fact. "A daughter is a "child" like "son ". No religious rule therefore can change her status. The Nepalese law in this connection is therefore even inconsistent with the rules of "*Mimansa*" (interpretation) under Hindu jurisprudence. Prohibition on independent identity of women is the main problem of Nepalese women.

Summary of Key Values Prevalent in Nepal

"*Mitakcshara*" one of the schools of Hindu jurisprudence has given absolute power to the husband in the property. This school even defines wife as the property of husband."*Dayabhaga* " another school, however, denied women as the property of husband. "*Mitacshara*" does not merely define women as property, but also take woman as commodity. Not only Eastern civilization but also as antique Roman civilization considered women as commodity rather than personal entity, that was why murder of women was not taken as a crime in the western society. "*Dayabhaga*" of the Hindu jurisprudence to some extent seems flexible to the status of women in society. However it's too not progressive in providing gender rights. The Nepalese law is heavily influenced by these schools, and as such it is not only gender discriminatory, but also caste discriminatory. Since, the law take general assumption to women as commodity, the treatment offered to women are sexually biased. The source of discriminatory approach is a defective value of marriage between male and female. This is reflected in existing legal system. As per this approach, marriage directs the personality of women. Naturally such ideology keeps women under their husband. The imposition of male dominance is emerged by this theory. That is why marriage is defined as an expression of man's dominance upon women.

Conclusion

Dalit women's problem has doubled edges. On the one hand, the issue relates to larger problem of social segregation and suppression based on the imposed caste, and on the other hand it relates to their conjugal life, where the husband is master of the life in all aspects. In the later case, the position of Dalit women has no difference from women from other castes. In the former case, the women's problem is rather a caste problem. However, the social segregation largely contributes to the vulnerability of invasion to the physical and mental integrity of Dalit women. The law does not affirmatively protect the Dalit women against vulnerability.

References

Bista,Dor Bahadur. *People of Nepal.* Ratna Pustak Bhandar, Kathmandu. 1996.

Bavisakar, Amita. *Development, Nature and Resistance: The Case of Bhilila Tribals in the Narmada Valley.* Cornell University, 1992.

Choudhary, S.N. *Community Power Structure.* HAR-ANANDA Publications-- 1993. (PP.22-30.)

Mallik, Ross. *Development, Ethnicity and Human Rights in South Asia.* Sage : New Delhi, 1998.

Mendelsohn, Oliver and Upendra Baxi. *The Untouchables.* Ed. The Rights of Subordinated Peoples.Oxford India Paperbacks. 1996.

Mohanty, Manorajan, Partha Nath Mukherji with Olle Tornquist . Ed. *Peasants, Dalit and Women: Democracy and India in People's Rights: Social Movements and the State in the Third World.* Sage, New Delhi. 1997.

Sangroula,Yubaraj. *Condemned to Exploitation: Trafficking of Women and Girls in Nepal.* Kathmandu School of Law, 2000. PP. 20-50.

Vanaik, Achin Vanaik. *Communalism Contested: Religion, and Secularization.* Vistaar Publication, New Delhi. 1997.

Part Two
Art and Society

Dalits and Performing Arts

Abhi Subedi

The contradiction of the caste-based society can be seen in the very process of relegating different roles to Dalit groups in the society. The greatest contradiction and the hypocritical foundation of the Brahmanic religio-aesthetic construct can be seen in the role of performances assigned to the social classes like the Damais, Gaines and Badis. Each of these castes has been traditionally assigned roles in the performance culture of this country. The main components of the performance are related to music, musical instruments, dancing and drama.

Dalit performances do not follow dialogical texts, nor do they follow any improvisations of dramatic nature. The interactive power of the Dalit performance is acquired through the dynamism of the moments and occasions. The recipients are those who recreate their thrills for the festivals or occasions like wedding, *rites de passage* or any other such moments. Dalit performance art does bring the community together, creates a melange of various socio-cultural practices, brings the deities and the humans and future hopes and present reality together. The theatre of the performance is thus a space as well as the psyche of the audience who wake up to a new reality of life, for example, when the performers create music, perform dances or present short plays. The most important performance in the hills is the music created by the Damai *Panchai Baja* band. But the contradiction is that a caste-created gulf separates the performers and the recipients. Despite all the closeness that people feel on the occasion when the performances are made, ensemble of musical instruments is played and dances are performed to the music, upper caste groups maintain a distance with the performers who are considered lower in caste, who nevertheless perform the most important role to reinvigorate people's spirits on the occasion.

There are many practices in the plains of Nepal too, which follow similar patterns as practised in the Indian rural areas like the Dalit performers coming to present dance-dramas, not too long in duration, on various happy occasions like wedding and birth, especially that of a male gender.

Groups of people and social classes who have been assigned the roles of performances, especially in the domains of music, dance, singing and dramatic presentations on different occasions in the ritual cycles, have for long been performing the roles as part of their caste privileges. But the privileges they have been perpetuating for centuries and even for millennia have served as the means in the hands of those who wield power through ruling and maintaining religio-cultural superiority to perpetuate an institution of oppression and domination in the society. The patterns of such domination can be seen not only in Nepali society but also in other countries of South Asia, especially in India where various forms of performance art and dramatic presentations have been the sole responsibilities of the class of people in the society who have taken up their roles as performers, which shows their caste groupings and their status in the society. The roles relegated to them are thus taken as their 'hallowed' professions in the society.

Ironically, performance culture and arts have been the life sustaining professions of people in different cultures. The minorities in the society and those who have for generations been denied any access to power and role in the administration and social works have taken up music, singing and entertainment as their main professions. Such groups abound in India where the caste system works at all levels of the society. The 'Gypsies' and minstrel groups in Europe and Asia always take up the performance culture by staying on the periphery of the central social norm dominated by the privileged or high caste people. The Gypsies performance culture is a matter of exigency, the principal mode of sustenance and survival. The tradition of performing art among the Gypsies has survived on the periphery of the metropolitan cultures that they encounter, and they present their performances under tents and open places, caravans and stages.

Thus the groups of people who play music and perform dances and plays are said to be ritually less pure in the caste hierarchy. But paradoxically, the people of the lower *varna* group having occupations with what they consider as defiling features perform music and dance at the time of the rites of passage and different ritually purifying occasions of the people of the upper castes.

Dumont believes that the logic of caste hierarchy is based on a synchronic ideology of ritual status not on the "historical processes of exploitation and discrimination".[1] But in the historical process and the genesis of the performance rituals, we find that the basic contradiction between the so called caste purity and the perpetuation of the

1. Cited in Mary M. Cameron, *On the Edge of the Auspicious: Gender and Caste in Nepal* (Chicago: University of Illinois Press, 1998) p. 11.

process of exploitation by relegating to the Dalits their roles to handle the performing arts and yet remain segregated from the mainstream culture dominated by the Brahmanic ideology, continues to form the basic pattern of domination.

The genesis of the role assignment dates back to the early times in the Indic culture. The inherent contradiction in the attitude of the twice-born or *dvija* or Brahmanic power holders by which I mean the whole set up of the Varna system and the ruling class of Kshetriyas, next in caste hierarchy to the Brahmin, becomes manifest in the Vedic culture itself. The genesis is very revealing. I would like to present a quotation of the legend of *Natyasastra* that appeared towards the mid-first millennium B.C. for making clear my argument about the inherent contradiction in the caste based society's performance aesthetics. Bharata *muni*, the author of *Natyasastra* tells the genesis of the *Natya* in this manner:

> Let the origin of the Natyaveda devised by Brahma be heard by you. O Brahmins, in the days of yore when the Golden Age (Krtayuga) of Many Vaivasvata arrived, the people became victims of lust and covetousness and were *engaged in rustic rites, overwhelmed by jealousy and deluded by wrath, wavering between happiness and misery.* Then great Indra with other leading gods submitted to Pitamaha (Brahma): 'We wish to have an *entertainment that would deserve being visible and audible. The Vedic discussion and practice cannot be proclaimed among those born as Sudra castes. Be Pleased to create another, fifth Veda, common to all the Varnas.'* Let it be so', said he in reply and then, having dismissed the King of gods (Indra), he resorted to yoga power and recalled to mind the four Vedas. He then thought: 'I shall make a fifth

Veda, entitled Natya with Itihasa. It shall conduce to duty (dharma), wealth (artha) as well as fame, shall contain good counsel and a collection of didactic maxims; it shall give guidance to the future people in all their actions, will be enriched by the teaching of all Sastras and demonstrate all types of arts and crafts. Natya will be its name'. Fully recalling to his mind all the Vedas after this resolution, the Holy Lord created Natyaveda, having its origin in and connection with the main Vedas and supplementary Upavedas by the holy Brahma, who is omniscient. After evolving the Natyaveda Brahma said to Indra: 'Myths and legends (Itihas) have been composed by me, put it to practical use among the gods. May this Natyaveda be *passed on to those among them who are skilful, learned, bold in speech and indefatigable'.* On hearing what has been mentioned by Brahma, Indra bowed to him with folded palms and replied thus: *'O the best and holy One, the gods are unworthy of the art of Natya because they are incapable of receiving, retaining, comprehending and putting it into practice. The Sages, who possess the esoteric mystery of the Vedas and are firm in the observance of holy vows, are capable of receiving, retaining and putting it into practice'.*[2] (My emphasis).

This extract introduces the most important point of the paradox I have been discussing in this article. The power of Dionysian revelry can be chaotic if it is not put into a form. Very interestingly, we can attribute the origin of the Greek drama to the Dionysian revelry. According to Nietzsche, the Dionysian artist is in ecstasies, or he is 'at once artist in both dream and ecstasies' but we picture him 'sinking down in his Dionysian drunkenness and mystical self-abnegation' and

---

2. *Natyasastra*, quoted in Natalia Lidova, *Drama and Ritual of Early Hinduism* (Delhi: Motilal, 1994) pp. 113-4.

through the Apollonian dream-inspiration he acquires a symbolical dream-picture.[3]

The gods' problems started with the very existence of the people engaged in 'rustic rites', and very interestingly, 'wavering between happiness and misery'. But in fact, they were overwhelmed by the power, and even the flood of the energy of life to contain which they were out in search of a form, a mode of the performing arts. They wanted to put that energy into a visible and audible state for which they needed a poetics, a canon.

When Brahma created the *Natyaveda*, he did not seem to believe in the strength and power of the gods to perform it. His admonition was like a warning that the *Natyaveda* should be handled by people who are 'skilful, learned, bold in speech and indefatigable' but not by the gods. The king of the gods confessed then that the gods were 'unworthy' of such performances and the sages who were familiar with the esoteric mystery of the Vedas were capable of using them.

The gods represented the dominating class, the rulers who did not have the worldly life and thus missed its power. The paradox is inherent in the *Natyasastra* itself, which is secular in character. For the same reason, *Natya*, which includes singing, dancing and all forms of performing art, was taken up by the Dalits in the Indic caste based social structure. Many marginalised groups have kept the Indian indigenous forms of folk dramaturgy and the musical performances alive to this day. The Nepali Hindu/Buddhist culture has kept the main tenets of the caste based Indic performance culture, which can be clearly seen in the role

---

3. Friedrich Nietzsche, Trans, Clifton P. Fadiman, *The Birth of Tragedy* (New York: Dover Publishing, INC.,1995) p. 5.

assignments within the Nepali Hindu based caste hierarchical order.

Another paradox is that the Nepali Dalits like the Dalits in the Indic socio-cultural structure are part of the cultural formation as strongly as the people of the upper caste groups. They are not alien nor are they travellers like the Gypsies or other visiting cultural groups. The Dalits form the integral part of the culture, and paradoxically, the roles they play within the system of the rituals is as central as those played by the priests. But a differentiation is maintained through what Mary M. Cameron calls 'material resource asymmetry and the perpetuation of privilege'. She believes that 'people remain dominated not through the force of ideology alone but also through the practices and techniques of domination... and the material advantage of the dominant'.[4] Dalits who have taken up music and performance present their arts as part of the tacit acceptance of the domination.

---

4. Mary M. Cameron, *On the Edge of the Auspicious: Gender and Caste in Nepal* (Chicago: University of Illinois Press, 1998) p. 51. Cameron in her book focuses on the status and position of women within the Dalit groups. In her very interesting analysis she examines the position of women within the Varna-Caste nexus. I particularly find her study interesting because she has analysed the problematic of the caste hierarchy and gender relations in a society where the position of women across caste groups bear strong resemblances with one another and the character of the male-dominated society shares a number of features when we talk in terms of the predicament of women in the society. To my mind, a strong analogy with the Dalit women would be the position of the African American women whose black community is, as Richard Rorty said in one lecture given at the Himal Association in Kathmandu in September, 2001, looked upon as a caste group by the white American society.

If we only take an example of the role of the Damai-music and the inevitability of the presence of the Damai musicians on important occasions in the ritual cycles of life of the Brahmans, Kshetriyas and other caste groups higher than the musical performers, we can see the nature of the contradiction between the roles of the Dalit performers and that of the caste-based society. The *Panchai Baja* is played on all auspicious occasions of the higher caste groups. In all the *rites de passage* of the Hindus like wedding, sacred thread investiture ceremony of upper caste group boy, known as *Vratabandha*, and most of the festivals in the calendrical and the agricultural cycles like *hile jatra* and *bethi Panchai Baja* is necessary. The contradiction can be seen when the Damais without whose performance no religious rite can be accomplished are given not only a role but also a space where to perform. They are not allowed to enter other spaces where the rituals are being performed. Carol Tingey rightly says, "In examples, such as these, the role of the musician could not be considered as either that of entertainer or status symbol, he could only have been fulfilling a ritual function".[5]

Gaines, the very well known troubadours in Nepali society have a very historical association with the culture of this country. They are like the singers of Serbia and African

The Dalit women do not play any significant role in the performing arts. The musical groups like the Damais and Gaines assign women their roles in the households. Except for a few cases where women play some light instruments, I have not seen women taking part in the performances. On the auspicious occasions when the *Panchai Baja* band is played women are not given any share, which reflects the sexual prejudice within both the society of the Dalits as well as those of the other caste groups in the society.

5. Carol Tingey, *Heartbeat of Nepal: The Panchai Baja* (Kathmandu: Royal Nepal Academy, 1990) p. 178.

countries who sing the saga of the nation, narratives of epic grandeur and the stories of the communities. The *Gaines* are basically singers who visit people's houses and sing songs about historical incidents, love, faith and battles. Their presentation and the style of singing evoke social drama the stage of which is the mind of every listener.

The representation of the Dalits in various other forms of performances has been the accentuation of their stereotypical roles as performers. Their representation in the broader social dramas, most prominently the cinemas produced by the non-Dalit groups of people is made in the already constructed 'discursive spheres'. By citing Goldberg, Robyn Wiegman says, "race and ethnicity are social constructions linked to the specific discursive spheres within which they are used".[6]

Some Nepali films have created social spheres within the film narratives to represent the Dalits' performing arts. In a film titled *Simarekha* a Gaine comes out singing the story of Bahdur Shah's bravery. Bahadur Shah was King Prithvi Narayan Shah's son who is said to have completed the task of the unification of Nepal in the 18th century. The troubadours evoke the Gorkhali nationalism and history in their performances, and the selfsame aspect is represented in the film. In another film *Jivan Rekha*, the Gaine represents the agonies of the daughter of an arrogant Rana aristocrat. Gaine's performance art is represented as the means of highlighting the feelings of pain and love in the film. In *Mayapriti* the troubadour expresses the nostalgia and the pain

---

6. Robyn Wiegman, "Race, Ethnicity and Film" in John Hill and Pamela Church Gibson ed. *The Oxford Guide to Film Studies* (Oxford: OUP, 1998) p. 161.

of separation in the voice of a soldier who is dying in the Nepal Tibet border after the Tibet-Nepal war. He sends messages to different members of his family in various ways. This very well known Gaine-song dramatises the entire social ethos and nuances of family relationships in Nepal. *Sarangi* or the fiddle of the Gaine is given the expressive dimension. In a famous film titled *Prempinda*, which is the filmed version of the play of the late great Nepali dramatist Balakrishna Sama, a Gaine is given a space within the narrative whose role is again to dramatise the pain experienced by the lovers in their forced separation. The Gaine is also given the role of a person who foresees the union of the lovers.

In a few films, like *Bhisma Pratigya* and *Andhiberi* the story tries to break the caste barriers and make Dalit girls fall in love with Brahmin boys. But the films are not bold enough to perpetuate the union and kill the Dalit heroines as solution. The attempt to subvert the Casteism in the cinematic performance fails in these films where the drama is very weak and the screen plays are always haunted by a sense of timidity, and they end up creating melodramas.

Dalits' role as performers as extended through the media of cinematography is presented as one of giving expression to the pain suffered by the upper caste characters. The films show the psychic dependence of the upper caste characters on the Gaines' singing, the melody of his fiddle and his humanity and kindness. But in the society, under the caste system the Gaines are socially segregated. This paradox continues to haunt the psyche of the producers, directors and writers involved in the production of the film.

Finally, there is one important point to consider. The performances of the Dalits in Nepal and other countries of

South Asia do not have any sense of conflicts as in many post-colonial performing arts in which according to Gilbert and Tompkins, "Ritualised forms of conflict--both physical and verbal--became an important part of the post-emancipation Carnival".[7] The performing art of the Dalits because of its very long historical association with the culture and polity of the nation, has remained part of the age-old culture of that area. For example, the *Gaines* sing from the repertoire of the history of the nation, a kind of syncretic secular form of songs and singing. The other group, especially the Damais have long been performing their roles as musical performers and dancers, whose performance as we saw above, forms the texture of the rituals.

Performance arts have strong folk base. The other very interesting feature of the Nepali Dalit performing arts is its rural flavour. In earlier times the performance of the musical bands like the *Panchai Baja* had purely attributive significance. The band is associated with the Damais class just as the fiddle *Sarangi* is attributed to the troubadours called Gaines. The Dalit roles are strongly maintained in the folk cultural and ritual practices. But with the growth of urbanisation, the roles of the Dalits have been taken over by the professional groups in the metropolitan areas. The wedding bands, for example, are no longer comprised up of the Damais in the urban areas. Therefore, Dalit performing arts survive in the rural areas.

The most important point to consider, I think, is the symbiosis that the Dalit performing arts have with the ritual and calendrical cycles of the festivals of the society, a fact that only reflects the paradox of the caste-culture nexus and the

---

7. Helen Gilbert and Joanne Tompkins, *Post-Colonial Drama* (London: Routledge, 1996) p. 80.

contradictions of the value system of the Brahmanic culture that has for millennia been sustaining a pattern of cleavage among the people of the society created to perpetuate a system of control and exploitation in different domains of the caste-ridden society.

But to assume that the Dalits have only been playing the shadow music to the Brahmanic society is to ignore the great traditions of theatre and dramaturgy that the Dalits have created especially in South Asia over the millennia, and their impact on the modern performing culture that is vibrant and creative.

Having said that, the dominance perpetuated by the creation of a culture that is based on the foundation of exploitation of the Dalits by relegating to them roles in the performing arts that suit the interest of the high-caste people best, as we have discussed in this short article, is an anachronism and therefore can not be accepted in the twenty-first century.

References

Cameron, Mary M. *On the Edge of the Auspicious: Gender and Caste in Nepal.* Chicago: University of Illinois Press, 1998.

Gilbert, Helen and Joanne Tompkins, *Post-Colonial Drama.* London: Routledge, 1996.

Lidova, Natalia. *Drama and Ritual of Early Hinduism.* Delhi: Motilal, 1994.

Nietzsche, Friedrich. Trans, Clifton P. Fadiman, *The Birth of Tragedy.* New York: Dover Publishing, INC., 1995.

Tingey, Carol. *Heartbeat of Nepal: The Panchai Baja.* Kathmandu: Royal Nepal Academy, 1990.

Wiegman, Robyn. *"Race, Ethnicity and Film"* in John Hill and Pamela Church Gibson ed. *The Oxford Guide to Film Studies.* Oxford: OUP, 1998.

Kali's Subaltern Images

Arun Gupto

God is not always a transcendental concept in religious beliefs. There are deities who can be conceived as immanent ones, those who are easily approachable in human imagination and faith. The transcendental conception creates a distance between god and man. God is revealed only through austerities, meditations or renunciations. In folk cultures especially, these immanent gods and goddesses even possess human attributes and are presented with common human follies. Transcendental concept of god-hood distances divinity from human beings, and they are basically ascetically, philosophically understood.

Folk cultures and ethnic communities have their own deities who are presented through folk cults, cultuses, rites, rituals and narratives. These deities are worshipped not only because they have supernatural or magical powers but also because they are accessible in and around the villages, lanes, ponds, trees, fields and mountains. There are abundance of these local gods and goddesses, symbolically, metaphorically, conceptually living and even dying with men and women around. Such folk or local deities are sometimes included in larger pantheon and at the same time the gods and goddesses of larger pantheon are manifested in local traditions. Indus Valley people before the invasion of the Indo Aryans were already worshipping some form of proto-Kali as a fertility and mother goddess. The Vedic culture took Kali into its own religious context.

Shiva's earlier form is supposed to be Pushan, the god of travelers and agriculture. Both Kali and Shiva are two of the major deities in the major Hindu pantheon. They have their folk forms with various names in different parts of South Asia. Shiva, one of the trinities of larger Hindu pantheon, is also presented as a local god in the narratives and rituals of folk cultures. Shiva can be understood as a local as well as a transcendental god. In Hindu belief he is the destroyer who annihilates the universe to construct it again. He, in this form, has many philosophical and theological conceptualizations, and at the same time, his role in folk culture is like that of a common man engaged in family problems, at loggerhead with his wife, smoking *ganja*, running errands with ghosts and goblins. Probably, all the divinities of a larger pantheon evolve out of local forms. These gods are basically seen thus in two forms, the canonical and the common. By canonical, I mean the major deities who have higher status in the pantheon, and by common, I mean who have popularity more in folk traditions or the canonical ones who have folk colorings.

Kali has her canonical status in the divine hierarchy, and she at the same time is one of the most popular deities of folk, village religious cultures in Nepal and India. She has her canonical, transcendental significance as the symbol of the force of time, as one of the emanations of devi Durga. She is one of the ten divine female manifestations, the primordial feminine energy, or the ten mahavidyas.

As a local goddess, Kali is a charismatic figure. Charisma is one of the interesting and dynamic features of Hindu religion. Charisma can be understood as a pervasive term.

The element like appeal, charm, magicality, and drama of rituals and beliefs are associated with folk traditions that create charisma in common religious practices. Such practices help break the monotony of religion's high seriousness. One of the causes of joy and charm of religion is the charismatic role of the deities in rituals and narratives. Religion does not loose its charm thus, in the minds of the common people. Philosophical conceptualization has its own valid place in religious beliefs, but divinities in their enigmatic roles in common ethnic cultures enrich religion with enthusiasm, enchantment, magic and excitement. Gods and goddesses as represented by the type of Kali suggest how divinity is not merely a thing of distance that can be approached only through suffering, penance, and meditation, but also can stand at handshaking distances. These forms of supernatural beings can come to your house, threaten you, cause diseases, bring misfortunes, solve problems, give blessings, eat your offerings, cry, laugh, sleep, and even die.

One can think of a god like Brahma in this context. He is more of a grave, and remote type of god. Among the major goddesses, Laxmi, the goddess of wealth and prosperity is more a local figure than the goddess of learning Saraswati is.

In comparison, Vishnu is remoter than his own incarnation Krishna and his equal Shiva. Kali has a subaltern status in many ways. She does not necessarily need elaborate rituals in comparison to what Durga needs. She can be pleased with even bird sacrifices (and even symbolic sacrifices) that in turn are used in family feasts. Villagers or common country people do not have to engage themselves in complexities of elaborate worship. One can go to a Kali temple in and around the village and pay tributes to her with flowers only, not necessarily with animal, bird and egg offerings, and return home gratified. Kali can be found with ease and comfort, probably more than any other Hindu deity except Shiva. She is conceived in many forms: as a goddess of disease in the form of Sitala or Hariti Ajima, as a tantric goddess in the form of Chinnamasta (or Vajrayogini in tantric Buddhist tradition), in forms of Chamundi the demon killer, as Dakini, the demon goddess, as Bagulamukhi with head and face of a crane, and Dhumbavati, the widow goddess.

It does not mean that other deities necessarily need austerities of ritual. The worship of Kali in many Hindu traditions is elaborate and complicated. Despite such facts Kali still is certainly more popular among majority of the Hindu communities than many of the other gods and goddesses. She easily represents how religion can work with the immanence of divinities. People think that she understands the language of the common people, their feelings and sentiments. That is why she is referred to as mata, the mother. Though she looks fearful and bizarre in the images and icons, her terrifying figure threatens the demon, yet again, she symbolizes comfort and protection to the devotees. In tantric tradition, Kali's mother image has more esoteric forms. Her terrible forms are the sources of attaining higher level of consciousness through common means and practices made at secret and lonely places.

Kali's subaltern status along with many such deities implies how religiosity is not just a rigid institutionalization, but also a system that functions for naturalizing the supernatural with the concepts like the immanence of god-hood. Subaltern is a common class project that allows religion to function on the margins, such as those represented by the peasantry, working class, and common folk, and the middle class country traditions. It is interesting to note that due to her subaltern images Kali is popular among the Dalit or the socially and economically repressed communities of Nepal as well as India. In such communities, she is revered as mother symbolizing protection from diseases, misfortunes, bad luck and many other ills of the society.

Kali temples are the most accessible places of worship as different from the temples of other deities. Amidst inter-caste religious discriminations, it is hardly conceived that a Dalit is disallowed to enter into Kali temples. There are instances, though few in Hindu communities, when such under-privileged people are forbidden to go to the temples, and on the other hand, Kali shrines are open to the people of all the classes. Dalits in general locate her with the activities of their daily life, and that is how she lives in the common religious minds of the Hindus.

References

Ashcroft, Bill et al. eds. *The Post-colonial Studies Reader.* London: Routledge, 1995.

Bharati, Agehananda. *The Tantric Tradition.* New York: Doubleday, 1970.

Bloom, Harold. *The Visionary Company: A Reading of English Romantic Poetry.* Ithaca: Cornell UP, 1971.

Hart, Jonathan. *Northrop Frye: The Theoretical Imagination.* London: Routledge, 1994.

Kinsley, David. *Hindu Goddesses: Visions of the Divine Feminine in the Hindu Religious Tradition.* Delhi: Motilal Banarasidass, 1998.

Mookherjee, Ajit. Kali, The Feminine Force. London: Thames and Hudson, 1998.

Mookherjee, Ajit, & Madhu Khanna. *The Tantric Way: Art, Science, Ritual.* Delhi: Vikas, 1977.

Stratton, Hawley & Donna Marie Wulff. ed. *Devi: Goddesses of India.* Delhi: Motilal Banarsidass, 1998.

Dalit, Music and Society[*]

Ram Saran Darnal

As mentioned in Bhrat's *Natya Sastra*[1], the saint Swati, inspired by the sound of the rainfall on the leaves of lotus, prayed the god Bishwokarma to make the same kind of musical instrument. Accordingly, the one faced drum was created. It is beaten with a stick. Since then it has been used as drum. According to *Sangeet Makarand*[2], *Mardal-madal* originated with the combination of the god of the gods Shiva and his consort goddess Parvati. Rudra himself lived on the right and Uma lived on the left. Thus the drum was born with the union of Shiva Shakti. According to Shiva *Damrudbhava*, Mahadev, God of the Gods, formulated fourteen formulae of Animadi grammar[3] from his *Damaru*[4]. It can be guessed from the double-faced musical instrument, that it may have been originated from Shiva's invented Damaru.

It is very difficult to say anything about the ancient shape of the drum as it is not certain whether it was related to *dunduvi, panav, damaru* or *dhak* of *dhaka*. It has become the

---

[*] This article is prepared by editor with the help of original informations provided by the author.

1 Propounded by Bhart Muni, 2nd-5th century.

2 Propounded by Narad Muni, 9th century.

3 The 14th Sutras of Vyakarana from Shiva Damarudbha.

4 A drum like small leather musical instrument originally played by God Shiva.

subject matter of research. About its ancient structure, music scholars have different opinions.

According to a proverb, after killing and eating the flesh of wild animals the early tribes used to hang their skins on the tree. Sound was produced from the hung skins after having jostled in the wind. Later they were inspired and covered an empty piece of wood with skin from both sides and made a drum. According to another source, the early tribes of the jungle cut the hollow pieces of trees and tied skin on both sides and the sound was produced from this kind of hollow wood. In this way, the drum was propounded.

Thus there exist different opinions about the drum. Anyway human race has made highly sophisticated and complicated drums today. In spite of this fact, developing countries of Asia, Africa, Arabia, and Pacific regions still continue to use their original and traditional drums.

From the early cultural periods we have strong connection with music that has become one of the major components of social life. It is said that in order to arouse the God of the Gods Mahadev, Brahma beat the Karatala and God Bishnu sang the sanctity song (Mangal geet). Rishis started playing Bina - a kind of stringed instrument. All the Gods started singing and playing the musical instruments in order to make Shiva happy. Being happy Shiva says: "I shall help him who serves me by music and songs."

We have an old religious belief which says that Brahma plays Karatal, Bishnu plays Sankha, Krishna plays Murali, Shivaplays Damuru, Indra plays Mridanga, Sarashwati plays Bina. The importance of these musical instruments is deeply rooted in our society with strong cultural and religious beliefs. This belief also proves that socially and even culturally musical instruments have become a kind of living force to lead social life meaningfully and another important fact is that whatever musical instrument that we play now are associated with Gods.

Historical facts show that Lichhavi and Malla period were enriched by the cultural richness where music had its own value. Different Jatras, and festivals used to be held where music was the central force. From the early historical periods the essence of music has been preserved by some groups who are the professional owner and preserver of the music in Nepali society. Damai, Chamar, Badi, Gaine Hudke are regarded as the professional artists in the field of music. Unfortunately, the caste system has degraded the value and the norms of the music preserved by these groups and has marginalised the cultural value into a mere cheap-entertainment.

Traditionally, the people who have given the name Dalits are the preservers of the musical tradition propounded by the Gods. So, there is a kind of linkage between God's music and Dalits. Indeed, Dalits have become the real preservers of the heavenly gifted music in our context.

Damai from the early periods is regarded as the caller of sanctity (Mangal). Their *Panche Baja* and *Naumati Baja* are regarded the most *Mangal Baja* in the Hindu culture. Specially on occasions like marriage, *Upanayana* and in *Bijaya Yatra* (Victory March) Damai and their musical instruments are essential. *Hudke* and *Dholi* are also the musical instruments of Damai.

While making Panche Baja and Naumati Baja, Kami, Sharki (shoe maker) Tamot and Badi provide equal contribution. Tamot and Kami and Chunara prepare the wooden/metal body of the instrument then Badi and Sarki (shoemaker) cover it by leather. There is mutual participation and a sense of community feeling.

Temples are the most sacred places for the Hindus where Damais play different musical instruments like Bano, Bijuli Bana, Ras, Dhopa Bana, Marpha, Sikhar Bana, Kahal etc. for *sagun* but these instruments are disappearing now because of the intervention of modern technology and modern life style.

While thinking about *Panche Baja* and *Naumati Baja* King Prithvi Narayan Shaha had provisioned the post of Nagarchi, which indicates the importance of the music in socio-cultural and political life. Unfortunately, the social status of the Damai has decreased in Nepali society. The upper class uses the art of the Damai in each sacred moment but at the same time the caste system has been exploiting the whole artistic norms. Within the same cultural pattern their exists the illness of caste discrimination.

Gaines who are also regarded as the Gandharva, are also the traditional artists of Nepali society. Particularly after the unification of modern Nepal, Gaine became popular for the *Karkah* (songs of victory and nobleness of the warriers and the Kings). Mani Ram Gaine was the historical figure during the regime of Prithvi Narayan Shah. Unfortunately (as he was a Dalit) written history does not much talk about him.

In the Nepalese society, Gaines have their own importance they have preserved the culture of folk tales in oral tradition. During the time of Dashain which is the most important Hindu festival, Gaines sing the *Mangal gaan* of goddess Durga. They are supposed to be the callers of Goddess Durga in the houses of the upperclass people.

Badi is another socially exploited group, which is also the professional artist group of Nepali society. The whole Badi family live in the musical environment, where mother sings the song, father plays the Madal and daughter dances. In this way the whole family lives with music, and it is only their source of income. But gradually, they started being sexually exploited by the upper class people. Later due to lack of financial resources the women were compelled to be engaged in prostitution which was entirely a social pressure. Society forgot the norms of music and songs performed by this group. While talking about the horizons of Nepali music we need to address about the rich Badi culture but we do not have essential materials to reconstruct their musical instruments, their songs, language, and dances. So there is a need of more research on the Badi culture.

Chamar is another group of professional artists of Nepalese society. Majority of the Chamars live in Terai. Being the professional musicians and artists, Chamars are the source of entertainment in the societies. In many *mangal* works Chamars are invited where they play their drums and perform dance.

Nepali musical environment is preserved by the people of the Dalit community. Their contribution is not socially dignified, they are treated as the mere traditional workers. We have not realised the value of their music as the living force of society. So, these socially exploited groups do not enjoy dignity as the professional artists.

In fact, Dalit artists have made their contributions at the different historical turns of Nepal. Bishe Nagarchi, and Mani Ram Gainey's contributions for the unification of Nepal during the regime of Prithvi Narayan Shaha was of great historical value. Hira Devi Gaine was probably the first female singer in the history of Nepal. She used to sing the victors' songs, and the songs about different warriors and especially of Mathvar Singh Thapa. She was one of the historical figures to come out from the family territory and sing freely at the time when women were socially and culturally restricted. She revolted against the tradition and patriarchal domination. Bakhat Bir Budhapirthi was another historical figure who for the first time composed the national music of Nepal, during the period of Prithvi Bira Bikaram Shahadev. About the year 2013 B.S. some Dalit women singers like Jaldanda Badini and Patili Badini from the far western region and Sakuntala Badini from Dang had become popular national singers. During the same period Khim Bahadur Gandharva and Brikha Bahadur Gandharva from Kaski Batulechaur had become national maestros in the field of singing. There are other Dalit historical figures too but the written history does not mention them. Except Bishe Nagarchi's short mention, no history book talks about the contribution of the Dalit artists for the historical formation of Nepal and the development of Nepalese music, folk songs, dance and the overall artistic scenario. It is because Dalit do not have access to the education system and those who possessed the education system, controlled the history and also controlled the history of the Dalits.

Indeed Dalits are socially, economically and politically suppressed people. This suppression is leading the cultural heritage of music towards a crisis. There is a need of strengthening the spirit of music in Dalit communities. They need social, moral and financial support; otherwise they will not be able to compete with the growing impact of westernization and globalization. To increase professionalism in music, to save our cultural traditions and to develop respect for the minorities and socially disadvantaged group, there is a strong need to establish the Music School in the country.

References

Darnal, Ram Saran. *Nepali Music and Culture*. Royal Nepal Academy, 2045 B.S.

Hans, Weesethaunet. *The Perfromance of Everyday life: The Gaine of Nepal*. Norway, University of Oslo, 1998.

Tingey Carol. *Auspicious Music in a Changing Society: The ?amai Music Of Nepal*. Delhi: Heritage Pub,1994.

Part Three
Voice and Representation

Voice of Struggle

Durga Sob

I do not know why people used to hate me when I was a small child. In the village, people used to hate me, in the school, teachers used to hate me. The most painful situation I used to face was my own classmates' hatred for me. I was living in such a world where everything hated me. Nothing remained for me, except my mother's love.

One incident that I never forget is, one day, - I think - it was so hot day - I was in grade five. I was extremely thirsty, and I went to the office where there was water in a clay jar and a glass was also there. I was in dilemma whether to drink the water or not, but I could not control myself. As I took the glass and was about to pour the water into the glass, one of the teachers saw and scolded me. Gradually all the teachers and students came outside. Everybody was scolding me, saying, "you untouchable, how dare you touch the water! Oh my god! You violated the very sanctity of this temple of education."

I was nervous, extremely nervous... I was sweating, saw everywhere dark shadows about to kill me but I did not weep - I don't know why? I ran from the school to my house. My mother was washing the pots. She looked towards me and said, why you came so early today, I did not speak. I just embarrassed my mother and started crying and weeping. I related every thing to my mother. She was sad and said that this is the rule created by the God, what can we do? For the first time in my life I knew the pain of being a Dalit girl. That was my reality and probably that was the beginning of my journey; the beginning of my struggle.

I was the only Dalit girl to study in the school. Our Dalit settlement was not aware of the importance of education. Our neighbour used to talk different things, because I was a student. My mother, though she was uneducated, was conscious about education.

My family structure was large and complex. The whole responsibility to handle our family was on the shoulder of my mother. In that remote area, being a Dalit women; my mother played the role of my father too. Her courage to lead the family became one of the everlasting encouragements to me.

I don't know why I became rebellious from the early school age. The environment of my school was not in favor of me and of almost all Dalit students. Teachers were also not cooperative, ...in spite of all these things, I wanted to be a teacher, and I wanted to contribute my society. When I was studying in grade eight, I started to teach the adults and children of my settlement. People used to back bite me, but I was bold enough in my decision. I started to convince the Dalit parents to send their children to schools. I was partially successful in that mission, consequently some of the Dalit girls are studying in different colleges.

Later, I joined (Seti) a project, which was focused on non-formal education. I used to go to the neighboring village to teach. All of a sudden, after six months, I knew that Seti Project awarded me as a best performer. It inspired me a lot. When I was studying in grade nine, I got chance to participate in curriculum board for developing the curriculum of non-formal education.

I completed my high school with good result from the same school where I was psychologically suppressed from an early age. This was my pride, and victory. Later, I continued my study. Facing the numerous obstacles like, poverty, upper class hatred, etc. I did my masters in sociology and became the first lady of my school to gain masters degree where I always used to suffer a lot.

Later, I joined to an International Non Government Organization where I used to get attractive salary. But I decided to leave it because I wanted to work for the Dalit community. So for the first time in Nepal, I, along with my friends established the Feminist Dalit Organization where I got my real ground to work and fight against the caste and gender discriminations.

After this long background, my intention is not to talk about me. I don't want to claim that I can represent all the women and mostly the Dalit women of Nepal because somewhere the situation of the women is still worst. But being suppressed Dalit women, I can represent them to some extent than the upper class women and male. Because being a woman I represent them, being a Dalit woman I represent our common destiny. My revolt against the discrimination is the voice of my community.

Although, the Dalit men and women are traditional artisans, they are economically exploited and constitute approximately 90% of the people underlying below the absolute poverty line of the country. Politically, economically and socially, women are exploited rather than the male. Dalit women are facing double suppressions, the caste and the gender discrimination. Our patriarchal tradition has blocked us from opportunities of education that is why we are always treated as ignorant beings. Very few Dalit women are educated but they have no opportunity in comparison to the upper-class women. If there is some opportunity that appears as sympathy. Sympathy syndrome is the most dangerous thing for the progress. We do not need sympathy, we want our rights and we are fighting for the rights of our community.

Most of the educated and uneducated people of other castes sympathize us. The educated women try to represent us in different fields but how can they represent us? How can they express our experiences, our plights, sufferings and moaning? So, we our self should be able to represent us, for that we need education that can uplift our position in a caste-ridden society. Our movement should be vested first to uplift our community and then to work for the society. As much as possible it is necessary to locate us in different places like politics, bureaucracy, and at the planning level.

I am proud of being a Dalit woman, and we should be proud of being Dalits. This is our identity, the need is to glorify it. We all Dalit women should have this consciousness of our identity, then only we can think about the common women's movement. In spite of the numerous exploitations, we possess the voice and that is the power. And now our voices are challenging the history; the history that has doomed our voice from the centuries in the name of untouchability. The women of my caste should try to know that they bear the half of the sky. But the male, including the Dalit male, occupy our place; Our importance is doomed by the upper class women as well as by the male within and out of our caste. Yes, it is true that within community women exploit the women which is a serious problem and that needs to be questioned. So, our struggle should be against the concept which tries to dehumanize us. Now, we should locate ourselves within this social structure and we should be able to fight for our rights. This movement for rights, is not against any particular community; it is again against the traditional , conservative thinking that tries to exploit the women and mostly the "Dalit Women", in our society.

The Search for Dalit Self Possession[*]

Khagendra Sangraula

A while ago I got the chance to participate in a Nepal Television program dedicated to Dalits. The organizer of the program asked me to talk of the status of Dalit life in Nepali literature. In response I said—Dalit life has been depicted in Nepali literature mainly from two angles. In the depiction done from the first angle, Dalits are presented as pitiable characters within Nepali society. In this section of literature, Dalits are given a *baraa bicharo* image, or an image of 'pathetic, pitiful creatures.' Dalits are poor, Dalits are miserable, Dalits are weak, Dalits suffer from a lack of self-esteem, Dalits are voiceless, therefore Dalits are suited for pitying etc.. The general ill fortune of Dalits depicted from the second angle isn't different from the image projected by the first. However, the Dalits depicted from this angle are called upon to raise their fists against the hurtful and exploitative social and political structures, which have reached them to their present hellish state. Rise, awaken, strike out, etc. This angle does not bother to enter the inner reaches of Dalits' present condition, or to describe or show the many dimensions of Dalit life in a social and historical context, and in an external and internal way. It only resorts to gross generalizations, and recommends that social and political powers be attacked all at once.

[*] Translated by Manjushree Thapa.

Thinking back later, I felt that what I'd said on an impulse during the television program wasn't too far from the truth. It is not my thinking that there are no efforts whatsoever to portray Dalit life through realistic literature. But I feel that this is not the mainstream of the literature which portrays Dalit life. Why?

Because the number of educated people in Dalit communities is extremely small. The few exceptional Dalit writers who have received the opportunity for mid-level or higher education, and who are involved in portraying the realities of Dalit life through literature, have not had ample, or appropriate opportunities to learn about the sociological and artistic methods which help examine life in deep, expansive and subtle ways. Because of the social and cultural condition of the Dalit community, it is natural that their journey towards effective and recognized media of expression be very long, hard, and full of struggle. Hence the Dalit who has for a very long time been forced to depend on others for a living has been debased into serving as the walking stick of others, into carrying the baggage of others, and into speaking, through their own mouths, about the experience of others.

In general it can be said that most Dalit writers view Dalit life from the two angles I wrote of earlier—the 'pathetic, pitiable Dalit' and the 'Rise and strike out, Dalits' angles. Most Dalit writers do not look at the experiences of their own community with independent eyes, or speak about themselves in their own voices; rather, they look at themselves with the eyes of others and speak of themselves in others' voices.

In my view it is not very far from the truth to say that writings on Dalit life by writers of the so-called upper castes are like the writings of social tourists who sit at comfortable *chautari* platforms and write while looking from afar at Dalit settlements. The social rules and cultural bindings of the ultra-conservative and inhumane Hindu caste system do not allow these 'upper caste' writers to enter Dalit settlements and houses and courtyards; entering Dalit hearts and psychological worlds remains a far more distant matter. In no sense it is attractive for 'upper caste' writers to approach Dalit houses in order to inquire about them. Rather this remains an issue of revulsion and rejection. By writing literature about Dalit life, writers are neither helped in their career nor do they increase their social repute. Rather, they must be prepared to become a figure of lifelong ire in the narrow and cruel viewpoint of ultra-conservative and arrogant society.

There is a police officer who I know; he is a regular reader of mine. For years he issued orders to have rods bang the heads of ordinary people who had, for decades, raised their voices for their rights and for their self-respect. Now he is retired, and is a great believer in lord Pashupatinath. One day I ran into him early in the morning in our neighborhood. He was heading to the Pashupatinath temple; I was heading to the newspaper store. In typical police fashion, he said to me very sternly, as though issuing a police order, "Dai, why are you writing so much about Dalits? Is there no other issue left to write or think about? Leave aside such sundry Dalit matters." He said this as though I hadn't been writing about Dalit life, but about the rotting corpses of animals.

I feel that the viewpoint of this police officer, who was throughout his career married to the motto of "Truth, Service and Security," is a representative expression of the entire police arena. The truth of the Dalits doesn't fit in the borders of the police's Truth, Service and Security; neither is there any need to serve Dalits, nor to guard their identities and self-respect. It is as though the Dalits are not human beings part of Nepali society, but something else—something mean, ostracized, and worthy of disdain. In truth, the police officer's viewpoint towards Dalits is the shared viewpoint of the entire state, which abides by the Hindu caste system, as well as of its controllers and operators.

In response to the police officer's request, I joked with him, "I was born to a lineage of Bahuns, but I married a Gurung woman and fell from my lineage *dharma*. My caste neither remained Bahun, nor did I become a Gurung. And so I'm also a Dalit. And where else should I stay but in my own home? Who else should I write about but my own people?"

The police officer was extremely displeased with my answer. For a few months after that incident, he wouldn't even greet me on the road, but would turn the other way, pretending not to have seen me.

It is not hard to catch a whiff of the stench of extremist Hindu caste discrimination in the bitter response of the honorable officer. From his view, I had disgraced myself from so-called Hindutwa purity, and had plunged from human dignity to transform into a Dalit. In fact it is not easy for a writer from a non-Dalit community who sympathizes with and feels for Dalits to think about and write on Dalits while ignoring the ostracism of the so-called pure castes. The anti-humanity view of the Hindu caste system forms such a strong iron wall forbidding the entrance of Dalit life into literature that ordinary writers won't casually dare to try to do so. Writers who dare to write about Dalit life must be ready to give up many things, just as I gave up the honorable officer's *namaste* and respect.

In the past five years, I have had direct contact with the Damai, Kami and Sarki Dalits of Parwat district. How I got there is an interesting story. A friend of mine operated an NGO in rural Dalit communities. The first time I went there was to speak on the development of human civilization. That meeting was attended by approximately four dozen Dalit men and women of different ages, belonging to all three castes. When I spoke of the creation of human beings, I did not claim that the hoary forefathers of the Dalits emerged from the feet of four-faced lord Brahma; instead I retold the story written by old man Darwin, that human beings had arisen from a certain kind of ape, under very specific conditions. I also said that the forefathers of those who consider themselves of upper caste, or pure, or superior, also came from the same ape. For the Dalits present at the meeting, that story at once became a source of excitement, joy, inspiration, disgust and fear. They also felt that they'd received an effective weapon to fight blindly faithful priests and village bullies who, telling the story of Brahma's creation, had never allowed Dalits to so much as raise their heads in self-esteem.

That story of our ape forefathers became the bridge which let me enter Dalit settlements and hearts.

I found a widespread terror, mistrust and hatred in Dalits towards all powers and organizations of the non-Dalit arenas. They hated Hindu priests because, acting on the orders of local bullies, they prohibited Dalits from coming close to temples. They hated village bullies because in the view of these bullies Dalits were not people endowed with human dignity, and hence they resorted to ritual cleansing as soon as they touched Dalits; and these village bullies were insatiable leeches who lived off the blood of Dalits. The Dalits also hated political parties because they had never done anything but spread false dreams and betray them. They hated the police and administrators because those in these posts did nothing but suppress and cheat them on the basis of highhanded punishment. Based on the essence of their experience, the local Dalits had come up with two formulas. The first formula was: they would never, from now on, serve as anyone's walking stick; and the second formula was: they would never, from now on, carry the baggage of others. The Dalits had formed a strong resolve to search for their rights and self-respect while remaining firm in following these two formulas.

The central story of my novel *Junkiriko Sangeet* is based on these two path-breaking formulas. But I found that even the Dalits took an oath not to be swayed from these two formulas, they slowly served as walking sticks for others, and contrary to their own wishes they began to carry the baggage of others. I saw them sometimes blindly turning into the walking sticks of NGOs, and at other times I saw them blindly lugging the baggage of political parties.

I have a few experiences in this matter.

After my novel was published, a proud Dalit youth leader said to me, "The novel is being read out loud to illiterate Dalits. They're very excited to find their villages' description, and their own stories and woes, written in a novel." I felt that this was the Dalit community's own reaction to my novel; it wasn't a reaction borrowed or forced onto them by any outside source. I know that this reaction did not come from the novel's ability to artistically depict the realities of Dalit life in a deep, expansive and subtle way. It was that there was no other literary book which, even in a crude and unrefined style, showed in such a wide-ranging way the many dimensions of Dalit life. In this sense one could say that my novel appeared good only because everything else was so bad. No matter what the case may be, my novel was welcomed by the Dalits, who perhaps felt, as the Nepali saying goes, that it was better to have a blind uncle than to have no uncle at all. There was a vacuum where there should have been reading materials, and the novel made do to fill this vacuum.

After almost a year's gap I went back to Parwat, the birthplace of the novel. When I got there this time, I felt as though I'd reached the middle of an unknown settlement, and was among unknown people. The expressions of many of my Dalit friends had changed, their inclination had changed, and so had thier speech. Trying to discover what fluttered through their minds, I examined their hearts and sensed that they had ignored their own experience-based formulas to never serve as the walking stick of anyone, and to never carry anyone's baggage; they had turned into someone's walking stick, and were carrying someone's baggage. In my earlier encounters, all Dalits were united into a single group. They were united in not relying on anyone till testing, through practice, who was a friend of Dalits and who was an enemy. Now, a hidden discontent and mistrust was spreading among them in regard to the NGO working in their midst. That NGO, which had at the start provided a lot of support in helping the Dalits coalesce, unite, and speak and fight for their rights had begun, as time went on, to display the inherent traits—or weaknesses—of all existing NGOs. The 'elder brothers' who ran the NGO lived outside the district, and the 'younger brothers' and 'younger sisters' who worked for the NGO spewed the most tedious advice without ever trying to understand the complex problems of the Dalits. Like Hindu priests, they only spoke themselves, without letting the Dalits speak. Or even when the Dalits got a chance to speak, these NGO brothers and sisters didn't have the patience to listen. The arrogance of the upper castes showed in their behavior. They were not friends and helpers to the Dalits, but distant advisors. It wasn't hard to see that their self-serving ways and their search for comforts and luxuries were making the Dalits increasingly mistrustful and put off by them. The distance and conflict between the Dalit community and the NGO was increasing. Even the Dalit youths who worked in the NGO would surreptitiously speak against the NGO when the NGO's 'elder brothers' were out of earshot; they were clearly dissatisfied with their work.

Unfortunately, this time around, I found that the voice of the Dalits had divided, and turned into three separate voices. The first voice was that of the NGO, the second was that of political parties, and the third was that of the joint organization of the Dalit community. Each voice was saying something different. The strange thing was that earlier, the NGO's workers used to turn up their noses at politics and at political parties. Hearing their arguments, one felt that NGOs were the supreme truth, and political parties were but supreme falsehood. However, these same NGO workers now stuffed their speeches full of complicated, jargon-filled political words and talk. It was very hard for me to make out whether their newfound political ideology was a new faith or a tricky cover to disguise the ills of the NGO. For such an ideological change , it is first necessary that there be a natural progression towards a change in thinking; and then this progression follows a complex process, and entails a period of sharp inner conflict. None of these processes were included in their stance. It was as though they'd fallen asleep the earlier night believing that NGOs were the supreme truth, and woken up the next morning saying that political parties were the supreme truth. As though in some magical dream, their conviction had changed form. And so, on one hand, the NGO's work was becoming unpopular in the Dalit settlement, while on the other hand, NGO workers were spewing forth grand ideals of revolutionary politics.

.The most incongruous part of this was that plenty of the communities young Dalit men and women who had learned a few letters, and who kept their eyes open and voiced their views, had found employment as the NGO's development workers. Earlier they used to fight for Dalit awakening on the basis of whatever meager lands they owned, on the basis of half-filled stomachs. But now they'd turned into development tourists who stayed in the district center, and sometimes visited their Dalit settlements disguised as strangers; they carried with them the baggage of development. Examining their expressions and listening to their talk, their first priority seemed not towards their community, but towards the protection of their income-giving NGO. Because of this, a cold war was taking place between the workers of the local Dalit organization and these development workers. The workers of the community organization were still committed to not serving as the walking sticks of others, to not carrying anyone else's baggage. The Dalit youths employed as development workers, however, resembled strange beings that swung, like the pendulum of a wall clock, between the NGO, the political parties, and the Dalit community.

Some Dalits had also left the village and moved to the district center after joining a political party. There was a party sign-board in the district center, and they stayed by it, guarding it. They looked like traders at a shop, which had nothing to sell. Was their party steeped in Dalit hearts and minds? The test of living practice had yielded no proof as such. Instead of inspiring Dalit youths who were scattered and lost outside to return home and become involved in the awakening of the Dalit community, the political party had dragged the village's conscious activist youths—who had been working under their own leadership—away from the village to the district center.

The workers of the Dalits' community organization, and the ordinary people of the area, were neither pleased that their youths had been kidnapped by NGOs, nor that they'd been dragged away by political parties. They complained that in both cases, their youths had, contrary to their oaths, served as the walking sticks of others, and were carrying others' baggage. Among those who were left behind, there was a serious dearth of people who had read widely, who could understand the jargon-filled speech of NGOs and political parties, who were skilled in debate and argument, and who had the guts to jostle confidently in a war of thoughts. That's why, as the saying goes, the low-quality flour of those who were skilled in talking found buyers; while the fine rice of the community organization could find no buyers.

In my last encounter with the Dalit community, there was some talk about my novel. Those who had earlier praised it now appeared to be its ardent critics. According to the points they made this time, my novel had neither a revolutionary policy nor a revolutionary program to take the Dalit movement ahead. Their complaint is valid; neither of these things are to be found in my novel. It is not a political manifesto on Dalit liberation, only a realistic depiction of the current state of Dalit life. The very expectation that the novel propose a pat formulaic solution to right life's many sociological problems was, in my view, not an expression of the Dalits' own experience, but an expression borrowed, or thrust upon them from outside the community. The astonishing thing was that the individuals who voiced such expectations were the very ones who were committed, through the NGO, to weaken the independent leadership of Dalits, to lessen their autonomy, and to make them turn to others for their survival. Yet in my novel they needed to find the path to revolution. Dalits who had vowed not to serve as the walking stick of others or to carry the baggage of others were now speaking as the walking stick of others, loaded with the baggage of others. They had spread their dislike of many useful aspects of my novel throughout the Dalit community, and were trying, with all their might, to hide the novel's criticism of their NGO's ill deeds, and to turn themselves into revolutionary heroes of the Dalit community. In fact the situation demanded that the NGO which had rooted itself in the Dalit community and had disempowered Dalits and empowered only itself needed to be given leave, and if it didn't leave of its own volition, to be chased away. But the Dalits involved in the NGO had cloaked themselves in the colorful garb of politics and become heroes—strange heroes who served as walking sticks for others, and carried others' baggage.

During the Panchayat Raj, in the name of making the Panchayat a garden of all castes, the rulers would haul up, by their hair, one or two Dalits, and place them on a seat of power in the make-believe parliament of that system, or as a Deputy Minister. These Dalits were mostly Biswakarmas. There are still, today, a few Dalits who have been hauled by the hair and placed in the Upper House of the multiparty system's Parliament: Dalits sheltered by the political parties, or by the palace. From their deeds and commitments, these Dalits seem to be placing the welfare of the Dalit community on a wager only to decorate the party or government; they are mainly working for their own private interests. For this reason it is not a great injustice to describe the few fortunate Dalits who step inside Singha Durbar as the walking sticks of others, or Dalits who carry the baggage of others.

Based on these all observations and experiences, one can say that the main problem of the Dalit community is the search for its own independent recognition. This recognition can be built on the foundation of the material and cultural offerings that the Dalit community has made from early on in order to keep Nepali society alive and beautiful. The presence of the Dalit community will be meaningful in literature only when Dalits are reflected in literature as their own walking sticks, carrying their own bags. This too must occur not from the pen of others, but from the pen of longsuffering Dalits. But again, this is in no sense possible from the pens of Dalits who serve as the walking sticks of others and who carry others' baggage. At this juncture, I feel that it is the primary drive of the writer who loves humanity to search for an independent image of Dalits awakening through class war and through the internal war taking place in the inner reaches of the Dalit community.

Who is going to accept this challenge?

Representing Dalits

Sanjeev Upretti

One honest gesture that all of us - including those who are writing for this book and those who will read it - can perform at the outset is that of admitting that none of us who are participating in this discourse of representing Dalits and actually Dalits. Even those among us who once came from Dalit classes and had to fight their courageous battle to acquire professional training against tremendous odds will realize that the education and the training that they have acquired has given them a relatively priviledged status of cultural and economic power that separates them from their brethren who wallow at a lower ground of socio-cultural and political powerlessness. The questions is what legitimizes our representation of Dalits? This question in turn leads to another: what is representation and what are its effects? Multiple theoretical positions are available on the subject. When we represent a particular group or a community - and in this case an economically and politically exploited group such as Dalits - we after all need to gather information and data about these peoples whom we purport to represent. We proceed by distributing questionnaires, interviewing the Dalits, recording our impressions of them, drawing our charts and tables of classification and amassing our databases and so on. On the basis of all such tabulation and organization of data a certain "truth" or "truths" emerge about the Dalits. Such truths emerge in the form of representations, or in the form of texts or writing; eventually it gets organized into a book or is re-presented in the form of a report or another form of publication. The question is what kind of violence we might be perpetrating upon the community that we seek to represent even as we classify them in our tables and charts and writings? By attempting to represent their multiple heterogeneous lived experiences within the discipline of bounded charts and concrete data do we reduce their lived multiplicity into the concrete, singular representations? If every representation is a violence as Foucault has argued, then what is the option left to us but to commit that violence as we try to represent the downtrodden since the only other option seems to be that of remaining silent to observe their suffering without intervening. Should we leave the task of representation to the Dalit community itself instead of trying to speak or write for them? In other words should we rather let the Dalits represent themselves instead of representing them through our grids and tools of analysis? The problem, however, is that the Dalits or the subaltern groups - as also argued by Spivak - cannot represent themselves. Dalits cannot speak within the web of historical and linguistic context within which they find themselves. Nations and civil communities have their own forms of permitted speech and codes of expression. Voices can find expression only by mastering the rudimentary codes of those socially sanctioned speech conventions. Certain degree of social civility and a mastery of a civil mode of address is required for the voices to acquire legitimacy. It is only by satisfying the demands of these civil and linguistic codes that the subaltern voices can find their way into the public sphere. Dalits are Dalits not only because of the exploited position that they occupy as the bearers of political and economic exploitation but also because they lack language or the discourse to make themselves heard. Their native "uncivilized" tongues fumble at the borders of civil discourse, producing only incoherent babble to all those ears that are conditioned to listen only to the "civilized" accents and modes of address. Within such a discourse of civil address that forms the borders of our national public sphere the voice of Dalits can only appear as an incoherent babble. Dalits cannot speak. What do we do when confronted with a people that remain mute within the discourse of civilty within which we conduct our great games of classification? Should we try to represent them by writing or speaking about them thus committing the violence of reducing them (Dalits) within the neat categories of our definitions? Or should we ourselves remain mute and reject our burden of representation by assuring each other that Dalits will represent themselves? In this context I agree with Spivak that even with the dangers of commiting classificatory violence we should not shy away from the task of writing about the people who cannot write or speak about themselves. We must try to continue to represent them with the purpose of generating public discussion so that it might lead to practical measures and programmes that will help liberate Dalits. The thing to remember is that we should interrogate our own position as "objective" observers and narrators of Dalits even as we seek to represent them. Only such a double movement - representing Dalits while at the same time questioning our own position from which represent - will lead to us to an awareness of the variety of the heterogeneous lived experience that form such a representative category or a label like "Dalits." Even as we tag them under the term "Dalit" we should remember that various heterogeneous multiple experiences are subsumed under such a term; experiences that cannot entirely be mapped within the systems of representation. If we work with such a double consciousness we can make productive use of the terms "Dalit" by using this term for the strategic purpose of making political interruptions. In other words we can use the banner of Dalits to speak about important questions regarding their rights and privileges and help form effective strategies to improve their lot. This is to say that we can and should represent Dalits while remaining actively aware of the pitafalls of our own position from which we try to represent them. It is only through such a politically sensitive representation that we - the non Dalits - can hope to improve the fortunes of those who, unlike us, are condemned by history, to be where they are right now, at the ghostly margins outside our rituals of civility. However, there is an even more important task that awaits us: a task that has less to do with abstract theorization and more with the concerns of practical strategy at specific locations. It is not enough that we speak for Dalits who cannot speak for themselves; we should rather work as intellectuals, social workers and as professionals to create communicative situations or public forums where the members of Dalit communities can come and speak for themselves. Such forums can take various shapes including participatory programmes organized by NGO(s) and INGO(s) as also talk programmes in radio and television. The role of the social worker or the non-Dalit professional should be that of preparing the ground, of creating a space within the public sphere where Dalits can come and speak in their own voices instead of speaking in voices and accents sanctioned by civil discourse. As they to speak in a "civil" language, following its grammar and vocabulary Dalits are reduced to silence or to the powerlessness of an incoherent babble. The thing to do is to work towards finding a space for them from where Dalits can speak in a voice that is their own, without shame, without guilt, without any debilitating awareness that their "Dalit-ness" somehow makes their speech inferior or deficient.

Rural Dalit Women and Work: The Impact of Social and Economic Change

Mary M. Cameron

The context in which the daily work lives of Nepal's rural Dalit families in the far western part of the country (the site of the author's research) must be understood is that of their poverty. The vast majority of families lack the most vital and powerful agrarian resource – land – and that lack is the result of historical and ongoing landholding and labor practices that have been transforming Dalit families over the past century. Consequently, the base of low-caste economy rests not directly in land, but in Dalit's artisan and labor skills, and even more importantly, in the kinds of relationships they maintain with families of caste higher than them. For it is those relationships, locally called *riti-bhagya* (the more familiar South Asian term is *jajmani*) which, in the ideal case of unchanged social and ecological landscapes, provide food security for Dalit families, and which, in the state of resource decline, forestall complete eviction from a stable livelihood. What are the dimensions of Dalit women's position in family-based subsistence? What kinds of work do they do, what value is placed on that work, and how does it effect gender relations in the low-caste family?

Nepali women's inheritance rights are based on national law (predicted to change, and be successfully implemented, before the decade is out) and local custom. Like most women throughout Nepal (and I speak of a general pattern, not a monolithic practice), women of low caste do not inherit landed property, not even the small infertile parcels of hard-won family land. Nor do they inherit the husband's family's patrons, a 'resource' more common than land to Dalit families, and one which is the right of sons to inherit. Many women's situations are worsened by their lack of education, by the health care needs that so many rural Nepalis face, and, for Dalits, rules of untouchability and grinding poverty.

As we often find for women's work in rural patriarchal societies like those of Hindus, the ideological or prestige value of the work women do is inconsistent with the work's instrumental value. For example, while high-caste women are the main provisioning farmers of the family, doing the bulk of agricultural (as well as domestic) work, they retain little power over the allocation of their labor or the fruits of that labor. Neither can they control inheritance of the land they farm, which devolves to the father and husband's patrilineal heirs. What we find in Dalit families, though, is a slightly different situation with respect to women. Dalit women exhibit greater control over the products of their labor. Still, since they often work for others, they do not control the land they farm.

Throughout Nepal, farmers and their dependents are affected by the erosion in land tenure relations, due to land reduction and scarcity, over-partitioning in an increasingly urbanizing country, devaluation of land due to civil unrest, and claims of ownership or sales that have gone awry, sowing distrust and disharmony among families. All of these pressures and stresses are felt within the cultural fabric, and are experienced even more severely for women of low-caste. Their gender denies them legal rights, and their caste denies them social ones. Their situation is unique among social groups in Nepal, and their comparison with women of upper caste requires careful attention to all factors. Low-caste women are in a position to be less subjected to patriarchy than women of upper caste, as in the absence of the patriarchal ideology that supports patrilineal land inheritance among the landowning high castes. Offsetting this marginal gain in equality, though, is extreme poverty, illiteracy and the social stigma associated with their caste.

For Dalit women, their daily agricultural, artisan and domestic work is shaped by and experienced through their gender and their caste. Because of their low-caste status and their economic vulnerability, Dalit women have functioned as handmaidens to the community's changing economic needs. Over the past century, they have experienced significant change in the kinds of work they perform, the groups for whom they work, and the types and quantities of remuneration they receive. The history of Dalit women's labor has been a gradual replacement of primarily artisan-related production with a variety of paid agricultural and nonagricultural work. The negative consequences of becoming free laborers in the agricultural economy include the breakdown of secure inter caste patron-client relationships and their replacement by informal and daily-wage labor in the context of increasing poverty. These are balanced against the positive social consequences of such changes for Dalit women, which include economic power in their homes and their communities, and which are tied to their role in acquiring rental land – called *maatya* -- for farming. A complex of many factors contribute to a woman's assertions of maatya-based power, including but not limited to family composition, land availability, the woman's own political, cultural and social skills, and the support of her sons.

In the context of social contracts involving the material dimensions of life in the mountain farming communities of the far west, gender changes have wrought changes in labor allocation and labor value in rural Nepal. The socioeconomic forces influencing these labor transformations operate locally, regionally, and internationally. The effects of labor transformations are present in those practices that serve to reproduce the social order of caste and gender hierarchy, as well as those practices that attempt to contest those hierarchies. To understand the present conditions of Dalit women's labor, we must first remember that historically, gender and caste relations have changed over time. While one could argue that caste restrictions have 'relaxed' over the past half- century in Nepal, other changes in Nepal's social history render caste relations ever more class (as wealth and education) controlled.

The most significant causes of change in Dalit women's productive work in the more recent period are male migration to India, competition from mass-produced goods, decreased supply of raw materials used in Dalit artisan production, decreased land market with consequent decreased formal and informal land ownership and increased land rental, changed norms for women's work, and an influx of outsiders into the area. While covering each of these factors individually is an extensive project (and I refer the reader to my full-length ethnography on the topic, *On the Edge of the Auspicious: Gender and Caste in Nepal*, 1998), a brief discussion of a few of the more immediately dynamic factors will provide a glimpse of the social vibrancy of ever-changing rural agricultural life and the place of Dalits in it.

First, the influence of male migration is experienced daily in people's adjustment to the lack of employment opportunities and an increasingly absent male work force. Today, women whose husbands are in India must take on work for riti and non riti patrons to maintain their households' position in the patronage system. Second, after the mid- last century opening of Nepal's border with India, Dalit commodities have had to compete with Nepalese, Chinese and Indian mass-produced imports that have replaced many locally made products. Over the past two decades, Dalit families have been forced to depend less on harvest payments and other customary clothing and cash subsidies from high castes because decreased demand for their goods has resulted in lower traditional payments. The artisans most affected by these imports are the Sarki leatherworkers. In addition to competition from international market forces, there are internal barriers to Dalit artisan production, particularly the recent limitations placed by the government, and the impact of environmental degradation, the supply of raw materials that black smiths, basket weavers, potters, and carpenters use in their work.

According to elderly villagers, in the past untouchable women were more involved in caste-specific commodity and service production, for a limited number of families, than they are now. Their work was narrowly defined by their family's position in the riti-bhagya system. Female leatherworkers, seamstresses, basket weavers, and goldsmiths who were skilled in artisan production worked with their husbands and other adult household members to meet local needs. Dalit families owned little or no land, and the economic strength of the traditional exchanges in the riti-bhagya system precluded the need for Dalit households to provision themselves in ways other than artisan production. If Dalit women did work for non patron landowners, it was not outside their patron circles and was limited to work for the local rulers. In the contemporary period in Bajhang, untouchable female artisans are, like their husbands, experiencing competition from mass-produced goods from India, China and urban Nepal. Women are compelled to shift their productive activities from artisan to agriculturally related work on their own small rented plots or on the land of patron landowners. Today, women in one region allocated only 9 percent of their time to artisan work, while three times that amount of time was spent in agricultural production, usually on a patron's land.

The list is long of the work that Dalit women do in rural Nepal. Such work includes artisan production like potting, weaving bamboo baskets, sewing clothes, and doing all the preliminary preparatory work for these, as well as the finishing work, such as delivering the products. Agricultural and daily domestic work that Dalit women do in addition to artisan work includes: threshing rice, wheat and millet, chopping wood, carrying heavy sacks of grain from the threshing floor to the home for storage, hauling slate for roofing, collecting firewood, carrying water, digging fields and preparing them for planting, carrying manure to the fields, and even house construction. The only job now unconditionally monopolized by men is ploughing. What is important to remember is that a large percentage of Dalit women's work is done for patron families, and their contribution to maintaining good and reliable relations with the patrons is enormous.

The rural economy of the far west integrates marked differences between women and men of low caste, in the allocation of time to productive activities; still, the complementarity of those differences leads to sustained subsistence provisioning in the Dalit household. We see these work arrangements most clearly in family farm production, riti-bhagya based labor, and wage labor. While Dalit women in the communities studied spent most of their productive time in agriculturally related work (68 percent), their husbands spent nearly the equivalent amount of time working in artisan production and outside income generating work (74 percent). This indicates a flexibility and complimentarity of women's and men's work in family provisioning greater than that found in upper caste households (where men's leisure time was found to be more than two times that of the women in the family).

Conclusion

What I hope this brief description of Dalit women's work conveys is how clearly the labor dimensions of gender relations are significantly mediated by caste in the households of far western Nepal. Caste and gender are the two most important factors contributing to the dynamics of subsistence provisioning in the context of harsh poverty and social discrimination. It is impossible to determine which barrier will be hardest to remove – that of poverty, that of caste discrimination, of that of gender inequality. What is certain is that the process must begin, and must make progress as rapidly as possible, so that future generations can know more opportunities and greater human rights than the older generations.

References

Cameron, Mary M. *On the Edge of the Auspicious: Gender and Caste in Nepal.* Chicago: University of Illinois Press, 1998.

Brief Introduction of the Writers

Abhi Subedi, Ph.D.: Dr. Subedi is professor and Head at the Central Department of English Tribhuvan University. He is one of the renowned poet, critic and writers in Nepal. His articles about art, culture, theatre and performance art are published in national and international journals. He is the president of the Nepal Centre of the International Theatre Institute (ITI). Pro. Subedi has over a dozens books to his credit.

Arun Gupto, Ph.D.: Dr. Gupto teaches at the Central Department of English, Tribhuvan University. He is a prolific writer on cultural studies, postcolonial subjects, religion and art. He is currently engaged in a study of Goddesses of Kathmandu valley. He has also directed and staged plays.

Bidya Nath Koirala, Ph.D.: Dr. Koirala is the reader at Central Department of Education, Tribhuvan University. He worked as a research officer at Research Centre for Educational Innovation and Development (CERID). Most of his research findings, especially in the field of education, have become helpful to government, and non-government sectors. He is a renowned educationist in Nepal.

Durga Sob: Mrs. Sob is one of the Dalit women activists in Nepal. She is the president of Feminist Dalit Organization (FEDO), which is the only organization of its type in the whole nation, which represents the Dalit women, and works for the upliftment of the Dalit women at a larger scale. She is also the president of Dalit NGO Federation (DNF). She has presented papers in national and international conferences and published many articles in different national and international journals.

Hira Vishwakarma: Mr. Vishwakarma has 19 years of experience working with different International Non-Governmental Organizations. He has been working with Dalit communities in Nepal. He has written various articles on Dalit and development issues which are published in various national dailies. He has also contributed personally and professionally for the birth and growth of leading Dalit NGOs in Nepal. During his student life he worked as an active Dalit activist.

Jit Gurung Ph.D. Dr.Gurung is a sociologist with interest on the day-to-day life situations of the Dalit and other disadvantaged groups in Nepal. Due to his interdisciplinary background, his research activities are very diverse. He finds himself equally at ease with research activities in the natural resource management and in the social sciences. Dr. Gurung is currently an advisor in DANIDA's Human Rights and Good Governance Advisory Unit (HUGOU).

Khagandra Sangraula: Mr. Sangraula is one of the renowned and widely read writers in Nepal. His contribution to Nepali literature is overwhelming. Most of his literary works including his famous novel *Junkiri Ko Sangeet* are the strong works for raising and articulating the voices of the marginalised communities. He has been writing as a columnist in different national newspaper, magazines and journals. He is a social critic.

Krishna B. Bhattachan, Ph.D.: Dr. Bhattachan is a lecturer and former Head of the Central Department of Sociology and Anthropology at Tribhuvan University. Dr. Bhattachan has jointly edited several books including *NGO, Civil Society and Government in Nepal* (2001), *Gender and Democracy in Nepal* (2001), and *Developmental Practices in Nepal* (1997). He has published numerous articles in books, journals, newspapers and magazines published from Nepal and abroad. Dr. Bhattachan has recently led a research team on *Existing Practices of Caste-based Discrimination in Nepal* for Action Aid-Nepal.

Mary M. Cameron, Ph.D.: Director, Women's Studies Center, and Associate Professor of Anthropology, Florida Atlantic University, USA. For over twenty years, she has been working in Nepal, specially focused on the issues of Dalit women and families. Her widely read book "*On the Edge of the Auspicious: Gender and Caste in Nepal*" theoretically links gender and caste hierarchy within rural Nepal and at the same time describes the multiple issues that are of concern to the Dalits of Nepal. Currently she is conducting research on Ayurvedic Medicines in Nepal.

Prabodh Mani Devkota: Mr. Devkota teaches at the Central Department of English, Tribhuvan University. He is also a journalist. Since a long time he has been working with the marginalised communities in Nepal, with special interest of bringing the marginalised voices into the mainstream media. Devkota is the author of the forthcoming book *Power Politics* *and Education: A System Analysis of Nepal.* His articles on postcolonial subjects, and the issues of minorities can be seen in different magazines and newspapers. Mr. Devkota has also presented papers in different national and international seminars.

Ram Saran Darnal: Mr. Darnal is one of the renowned musicologists of Nepal. He has contributed in recording the history of music in Nepal and published dozens of books on music and art. He is the founder of "Modern Orchestra" in Nepal and is involved with number of art and music institutions. He is also one of the members of Royal Nepal Academy. Mr. Darnal is synonymous to the music in Nepal.

Sanjeev Upretti: Mr. Upretti is a lecturer at Central Department of English Tribhuvan University. Mr Upretti is a prolific writer on cultural studies, the effect of globalization and the postcolonial subjects. His articles can be seen in different national and international journals, magazines and books.

Yubaraj Sangroula: Mr. Sangroula is the Director of Kathmandu School of Law. He is a practicing lawyer. *Jurisprudence and Legal Theory and Condemned to Exploitation* and *Trafficking of Women and Girls in Nepal* are two books authored by the Mr. Sangroula. During professional career, the writer has represented several public interest litigations directly related to the civil liberties of people. The representation of ***Chamar*** case in the Supreme Court was the civil liberty case of ***Dalit*** community, where the Supreme Court has made a positive intervention.

Index

ISBN 99933-384-0-